Loving Praise

"What I love most about this guide is that it ***validates the thoughts and fears of a mom***, with loving examples which empower readers as they encounter the daily challenges and emotional struggles of being a caregiver. I found the strategies to be practical to digest and implement. Being a mom is the most important job indeed; I'm thrilled to have this bible at my fingertips."

SIVAN FRANK, LMHC, LPC, Adjunct Lecturer CUNY and Mommy
www.SivanTherapy.com

"Jasmin's effortless charm and profound insights infuse every page of this incredible little gem of a book, where ***she somehow manages to both comfort and challenge the reader in each chapter***. I especially love her focus on self-care and the tools she provides to combat the drama and overload of modern parenting. I'm glad I didn't let the 'Mommy' focus dissuade me. Be prepared to be inspired!"

SCOTT DOTY, Founder and CEO of
Brainstorm Tutoring & Arts *and* DADDY!
www.StormTheTest.com

"*Extraordinary Mommy* is beautifully written, with raw emotional content and practical lessons aimed at encouraging any parent who wants to be the best version of themselves. ***As Jasmin puts it, "It's okay not to know what to do,"*** so letting go of the need to control, knowing that every day is going to be different, is okay. This is such an important theme for all mothers, and one that has empowered me as I learn alongside my three children. Refreshingly honest and inspiring, *Extraordinary Mommy* is a must-read."

JOANNA LANDER, LSW, Dietetic Student and Mommy

"As an entrepreneur who is passionate about both my career and parenthood, I wanted to learn ways to be an amazing mom while also balancing my business. *Extraordinary Mommy* has helped me to feel confident in my ability to parent in a way that I believe is best for my family by giving me useful tools for how to approach our life as new parents. For example, now I allocate work or family time, and put my phone on silent when I'm with my daughter so that the time I spend with her is of the utmost quality. I also ***prioritize my own well-being without*** [illegible] ssages to my husband that whenever a [illegible] does the book say about that!?'"

[illegible] O of Beaumont Etiquette and Mommy
[illegible] nontEtiquette.com

"*Extraordinary Mommy* warmed my heart. I didn't expect to feel flooded with emotions before reaching the first chapter. I love the way Jasmin connects her "mommy" lessons with personal experiences and her own mother's advice. ***Her words are relatable and inspiring, and not just for mommies, but for all caretakers of young children!***"

RENEE O. LEVINE, D.M.D, Dentist and Mommy
www.ReneeDmd.com

"This book has helped me shift my perspective when I am feeling impatient or frustrated with my kids. The ***two simple phrases, 'At least' and 'I get to' are my quick reminders to be grateful***, like: 'At least we are all healthy' and 'I get to deal with my daughters' backtalk because I am blessed with healthy daughters who have preferences.' I recommend this book to moms of all ages. Its format is easy to read, with succinct summary points at the end of each chapter for a quick review. If you are looking to create fulfilling, mutually respectful, and loving relationships with your children, this book is a MUST read."

AMY SABACH, MD., Radiologist Physician and Mommy

"*Extraordinary Mommy* is filled with wise, helpful, and perhaps most importantly, totally doable practices for mothers. Jasmin offers easy-to-use tools and ***strategies for real-life moms needing peace, calm, and centering***—along with a dash of compassion—comes from her own experiences as both a mom and a therapist. This is an excellent and much needed book. I'm so grateful Jasmin wrote this easy to read guide!"

ILENE S. COHEN, PH.D., author of *When it's Never About You: The People Pleasers Guide to Health, Happiness and Personal Freedom* and Mommy
www.DoctorIlene.com

"Jasmin's story of triumph and her mother's legacy ***helped me tap into a source of strength that I didn't know I possessed—especially when I'm feeling less energetic or patient with my kids***. The anecdotes and examples she shares are wonderfully broken down into manageable bite-size pieces that feel very clear and simple. Most of all, when I feel 'mommy guilt,' I remind myself of Jasmin's words that mothering *is* a very hard job, and that *quality of presence* is the most valuable gift I can ever give my family."

MORAN LEV-ARY GOLDSHMIDT, MS, CCC-SLP
Multilingual Pediatric Speech Pathologist and Mommy
www.SpeakUpBilingual.com

EXTRAORDINARY *Mommy*

A LOVING GUIDE TO MASTERING LIFE'S MOST IMPORTANT JOB

The 10 Secrets to Raising Exceptional Kids while Staying Relaxed, Effective, and Connected

Jasmin Terrany, LMHC

LIVE, LAUGH, LOVE PUBLISHING

Extraordinary Mommy
A Loving Guide to Mastering Life's Most Important Job
Be Extraordinary Series: Volume 2
by Jasmin Terrany, LMHC

www.JasminBalance.com
Published by: Live, Laugh, Love Publishing

Developmental Editor: Nora Martin-Cooley
Copyeditor: Cindy Walker
Copyediting/Proofreading: Deborah Mokma
Title/Cover Copy Consulting: The Title Tailor
Book Consultant: Ilene S. Cohen, PhD
Cover Design: Albert Edison Inc.
Book Design: Book Savvy Studio

Library of Congress Control Number: 2018905289

ISBN: 978-1-7321328-0-1

First Edition
Printed in the United States of America

To My Daddy

Although it seems that my childhood memories highlight Mom, I know your constant presence, unconditional support, and loving acceptance helped establish our peaceful and open home—the beautiful foundation of my life. Thank you for always being there.

Watching you help raise my kids has given me a whole new respect, love, and appreciation for the person you are and the role you play in my life. Perhaps it is our destiny that now I get to "remember" you as a parent through watching you parent my children.

I love you forever.

Love,

Jazzy

Acknowledgements & Gratitude

My extraordinary husband Matteen, thank you for being my rock. Choosing you was the most important decision I've ever made. We had no idea what life would throw our way, and I am continually inspired by your ability to handle it all. The way you take care of me and our family is beyond words. I look forward to continuing this beautiful journey of life with you as my partner. I love you forever.

Our children, Zen and Liv, you will never know the depth of my love for you until you have your own children. Until then, I promise to forever try to show you. You bring more joy, learning, and love into my life than I ever imagined. I love you with every cell in my body, with every ounce of my being.

My brother Zak, you never cease to amaze and inspire me. I am so grateful to go through this journey with you and feel so blessed that you chose the most incredible wife possible. I love you and Carolina more than you'll ever know.

My dearest soul friend Nora, thank you for revising this book with such care and dedication. I'll never forget the first draft, my excitement and dismay when you told me it had to be rewritten! I love you.

To my beloved friends and family, near and far, you know who you are. I am thinking of you right now. I feel such a tremendous gratitude knowing you are there. Always know that I will be there for you too. My life is beautiful because you are in it. I love you with all my heart, never forget that—because I won't.

Contents

Introduction

Meet Betsy

Learn of her extraordinary life ~
lived, lost, and loved.

I could feel the tears well up in my eyes. "Breathe deeply," I told myself, as I pushed the cart through the supermarket. "Hold it together. No one will notice. *You're okay.*"
But as I looked up, she caught my eye and said softly, "Let's go back to the car honey."

"I'm okay," I responded, feeling my body tense up as I guarded my heart.

I took one more step toward the vegetable aisle, but then turned back to her. "Fine." I left my shopping cart and bolted for the exit, tears pouring down my face as I ran to the car. I felt embarrassed. I didn't want to cry. I didn't want her to know that it was hard. That I was overwhelmed. That I was struggling as a new mommy.

"It's okay, sweetie. Just let it out." She maneuvered herself across the car's center console to hug me, and I let her. It felt so good. Amidst my sobbing, a feeling of gratitude came over me. She wasn't afraid of my pain. She understood. It *was* hard, and it was okay.

In that moment, I didn't have to be "Mom." I had a blessed opportunity to be a little girl once again, one who gained strength and comfort from her own mother. I relished that moment, and let myself fully experience one of the most powerful connections there is—the love between a mother and her child. I will always be grateful for that beautiful experience, that random afternoon. Especially since it will never happen again.

January 22, 2015

She was driving on the highway after leaving me a sweet voicemail about where we'd meet for lunch—but she never arrived.

Maybe her phone died. Maybe there was traffic. As time passed, I called my dad. He hadn't heard from her. We called the highway patrol and were told there had been a fatal accident, a head-on collision. The person going south had lost control of the car, crossed the entire grass median, and died instantly when hit by oncoming traffic. No further information was available.

My mom was going south. It couldn't have been her. Could it?

Then I received *that* call. I could hear him foaming at the mouth, screaming in agony, unable to breathe. "My wife is dead! My wife is dead! I want to die! Take me with you! I want to die! Take me with you!"

"Dad! Pull over the car!" I screamed as terror filled every cell of my body. "Where are you? Don't move! I'll get someone to you."

I frantically called his friends, since I was a four-hour drive away. They found him pulled over on the side of the road, screaming, crying, sobbing, shocked, frantic, and alone. There was nothing to do. Nothing could be done. She was gone.

All alone, I looked out the window at the clear, blue ocean as rays of sunshine kissed the gentle waves. How could it be so peaceful out there when my whole world was crumbling?

"*It's okay. You are okay. Everything will be okay.*" I could feel her speak through my soul as tears ran down my cheeks.

I felt it. I knew it. It was my turn. I was the mother now.

January 22, 2016

After the most heart-wrenching year of my life—managing my devastated father, my infant son, my marriage, my second pregnancy, my private psychotherapy practice, my social life, and an entire home renovation amidst my daily breakdowns—that terrible day was about to arrive on the calendar.

On the night of January 21, I hosted a conference call where extensive friends and family ate an ice cream sundae in my mother's honor while sharing stories and feelings about her and her passing. When I hung up the phone that night, I went to bed with a feeling of peace, as if a chapter had closed, never anticipating what the next day would bring.

Although the morning started out with a bit of a dark cloud over my head, when I felt a little rumble in my tummy before leaving the house I told my husband, "I think today is going to be the day."

And as the day progressed, so did my tummy rumble. It was happening. I couldn't believe it. I called my midwife and doula and made it home in time to fill up the tub. Three weeks early, and only an hour and half after arriving home, my baby girl made her grand entry into the world. It had been one full revolution around the sun since the day of my mom's departure and, to my shock and amazement, the most painful day on my calendar became the most divine. I still get goosebumps when I think of it.

My daughter was born on the first anniversary of my mother's passing.

When we called my dad to tell him his granddaughter had been born, he was driving to us on *that* road. When he picked up the phone and heard the news, he pulled over in disbelief as he realized he was at the exact spot where my mom had been when she left us.

She died at mile marker sixty-four, at age sixty-four, one week before her birthday. We had planned a surprise cruise for her sixty-fifth birthday, fifty people from around the world had purchased plane tickets to join us, the day of the cruise, her sixty-fifth birthday, became the day of her funeral. Everyone was already booked to be there.

Ironically, my mom began giving me books about spirituality and afterlife as early as ten years old, eerily preparing me for her transition. She often spoke of those who had passed, explaining they could connect through electricity and the flickering of lights—and right after our daughter was born, all the lights started flickering incessantly! Immediate silence and intensity of presence took the room as we stared at one another in deeply powerful disbelief. But we all felt it. Those lights had never flickered before; and haven't done so since. I know that my mom would have done anything to let me know "there is more to this life than we realize," and the events that day provided my confirmation.

As if that wasn't enough, my brother received his own gift. Months before, he had shared his excitement that the movie he produced had been accepted into the Sundance Film Festival. This was the second movie this twenty-nine-year-old, Harvard government major, had produced, and we were in awe that it had achieved this spectacular honor. Then he told me, "Jazz, you'll never guess what day the festival starts—*January 22, 2016!*" I couldn't believe it.

We thought that getting into the festival was unbelievable, but were completely dumbstruck when the movie *won the biggest award of the festival*—the U.S. Grand Jury Prize for a drama! Not only that, but its record-breaking sale was the biggest deal in the history of the festival!

A dear friend once told me that my mom was as close to a saint as you could get. I told him I agreed, but I had just assumed everyone felt that way about their mother. His roaring "No way!" reminded me that I did have a one-of-a-kind mom.

On the outside, she was strikingly beautiful. Literally ninety-five percent of the people who met her commented, "Wow, your mom is so beautiful! She looks so young! What a smile!"

Her jet-black hair, olive skin, and tall, slender frame were always accompanied by her sparkling eyes and glowing grin. When I asked her how she felt about having people react to her physical beauty in such a way, she humbly responded with, "The beauty they think they see on the outside really comes from within."

She was right. Her beauty did emanate from within. My beautiful mother was a being of love in the truest, most profound way imaginable. When people talk about old souls, they are referring to a soul like hers. She had deep wisdom and an understanding of life, with an inherent ease in the loving way she approached all people and circumstances.

On the flip side of her divine wisdom and stunning appearance, my mom was pure, silly fun. She danced at any opportunity, befriended any stranger (she got us invited to more than one random wedding), and went skinny dipping whenever she could. She also never hesitated to have an ice cream sundae to celebrate a Thursday afternoon.

My parents' house reflected all of this exuberance. It oozed love and fun. My friends jokingly referred to it as "Willy Wonka's Factory." The mailbox was a big pink heart, purple trim lined the outside of the house, and every post on the walkway to the front door, along with every cabinet in the kitchen, boasted a different pastel color. There was a red, illuminated "love" sign accompanied by hot pink leather couches and wall hangings full of hearts and ice cream sundaes. My childhood home gushed with delicious love. At the time, I thought it was ordinary. Weren't all homes overflowing with smiles and hugs?

It didn't seem strange to me. People felt warm, welcomed, and happy to be in our home. Yet, as I write now, as an adult, to you, a stranger, I realize it may seem crazy! Just as some homes have crosses, pictures of Jesus, or mezuzahs, my mom's reminders to live from love came in tasteful home décor in the form of hearts and ice cream.

Yes, in my eyes, my mom was as close to perfect as a mother could get. Was it annoying? Sometimes. She was a hard act to follow. Yet one of the best things about her was that she listened. She was open and humble. I could talk to her about my own insecurities and frustrations—even the ones I felt towards her. She was willing to reflect and learn from my perspective, always wanting to make sure she understood me. She treated me like we were fellow journeyers, often saying I was as much her teacher as she was mine. My mom was truly the best friend anyone could ask for, and I feel so incredibly grateful that she was my mother.

Looking back now, I know how rare it is to have had this mother, this home, this childhood. As a psychotherapist, I'm constantly reminded of how much our parents mold us into the people we become and the perspectives we have. So, whenever I doubt myself as a person, partner, or parent, I find peace in knowing that *I am a product of this woman.*

Since she passed, I find myself constantly asking: "What would mom do? How would she respond in this circumstance? What am I supposed to be learning right now?" The answer is always a resounding: *love.*

The intention of this book is two-fold. Primarily, it is an opportunity for me, as a new mother of two little ones, to reflect on my own journey into motherhood; a chance to identify and apply the lessons I have learned from my mom as I build on and refine the practices I was blessed to experience. Secondarily, it is an opportunity to share; to give other parents (or caretakers) the chance to gain from the wisdom that I so fortunately received.

As much as I personally feel grateful for my upbringing, I also have had feelings of guilt, or unworthiness—that I didn't deserve to have a mother like mine more than anyone else. In the past, these feelings have kept me from sharing for fear of boasting, because I realized I didn't do anything to *earn* this kind of love.

After her tragic passing, and upon writing this book, I now know that *no one* should have to *earn* this kind of love. We all deserve it for simply existing. My hope is to help all children receive this kind of love—through you—their mommies.*

There is nothing as pure and deep as a mother's love. Yet the challenges of life can make it hard to lead with this love. Let us strengthen our ability to do so.

Mothers have the most important job there is. Not only are we responsible for keeping other people alive, but we are motivated to help them thrive. This book is for all mothers, new and seasoned alike. It has nothing to do with your child's age, your religious background, if you are a working mom, or the amount of resources or support you have—the focus is on *fundamental principles to remember when you are in the presence of your children.*

With the full lives we all lead it is all too easy to fall into the *doing* of motherhood, and we can often forget the importance of *being*. How we show up for our kids is just as important, if not more important, than what we *do* for them. The *quality* of our presence is fundamental to the love they feel and the confidence they develop.

The quality of *being* is what differentiates great moms from truly extraordinary mothers; and extraordinary parents create extraordinary people. So, if any insight from this book can help another mother add another extraordinary person to this world, then the pebble of love has continued the ripple effect of my extraordinary mom—which makes my heart smile and makes the world a better place.

And, most importantly, thank *you*. Thank you for reading. Not just from me, but from your children. You are the most important person in your child's life. You are their first love. You are the role model for how to be in the world. Who you are and how you love them is the foundation of who they will become. How you talk to them will become their inner voice. Thank you for being the kind of mother who wants to be the best you can be—for yourself and for the ones you love most. Your children are blessed to have you.

* A *special note to fathers, "non-mother" parents, and other caretakers*: Since this book is about my mother, and I'm a mother, it felt most natural to speak to other mothers. Yet the principles discussed in this book are relevant to anyone who is responsible for taking care of children. My aspiration is that all kids experience the benefits of these parenting practices, and I hope you won't let the "mommy" focus keep you from garnering helpful ideas for use within your own family.

PART ONE

The Betsy Blueprint

10 Parenting Practices that Matter Most

As mother of two little ones, I can't claim to be an expert parent. As much as I do the best I can, I still have moments of exhaustion, impatience, and frustration.

Although I absolutely adore my little ones, sometimes I want to cry, scream, or even run away. I am human. Being a mom is hard. Think about it: In what other job do you not receive any breaks?

What I continue to learn through this journey of parenthood is the necessity for grounding principles. Just because I feel something in the moment doesn't mean it's the appropriate reaction. I find it helpful to have core values to which I can return, especially in challenging moments.

I was blessed to have had an extraordinary role model, and I believe that she left me so that I could share. I remember being parented by her, what it felt like to be on the receiving end of her patience, understanding, wisdom, and love. My intention is to paint that picture, to demonstrate how the quality of a mother's presence is the foundation of the home, and to share these fundamental practices so that all children can get the extraordinary parents they deserve.

Here is Betsy's Blueprint—the ten parenting practices that matter most.

CHAPTER 1

Embrace Change

The only constant in parenthood is change.
Go with the flow.

Lesson 1: Your life will be altered.

I hated my husband for the first month after my first child was born. Everything he did, or didn't do, annoyed me. What was going on with me?

Days would go by with no time to shower or eat, yet I would wonder what I *had achieved each day. I had no sense of accomplishment*. I couldn't check anything off a "to-do" list. My sense of success, as I knew it, was completely gone. Relative to specialized professions more highly valued by our society, taking care of a baby isn't universally understood to be "hard work." Eat, sleep, burp, poop. Right? Yet why was something so seemingly basic actually so incredibly challenging?

One of my biggest challenges was a lack of timeline with no breaks in sight. I didn't know how long the baby would cry. I didn't know how long it would take him to fall asleep. I didn't know how long he would sleep at night before I had to wake up again.

Sometimes I would feel a guilty sense of pleasure when my husband couldn't get the baby to stop crying. It was as if I needed proof that what I was doing was hard—for some unknown reason, I didn't allow myself to see it as challenging.

And because I didn't have anything figured out yet, it was all very uncomfortable. It's hard to feel unstable and unsure, especially when you are used to more predictable scenarios.

What would my mom say to that? "*You are in transition.*"

To further explain herself, she would undoubtedly add, "If you were in a new city you wouldn't expect to know your way around; you would see it as an adventure and get excited to learn something new."

This was the shift I had to make. I certainly didn't know my way around parenting yet. I had to let myself acknowledge that parenthood *is* hard work. What other job doesn't give you a break or let you sleep? In what other job do you bring your work with you to poop? It is truly exhausting to never have a moment alone.

Life changed. I had to adapt to a new normal rather than cling to what I had known. I was in transition. I wasn't supposed to be confident. I was new at this; it was okay not to know. As I became more comfortable with my vulnerability I made it an adventure to learn the "ropes" of parenthood—and continue to remind myself of this in every new phase we enter.

During pregnancy there can be lots of excitement in preparing for the baby—setting up the nursery, receiving gifts and attention, etc. Then the baby comes. After everyone congratulates you, they all go on with their lives, and you are no longer in the spotlight. Even though you are blessed with your most precious bundle of love, the excitement phase is over. You are in a new reality with no sleep, raging hormones, a saggy body, and lots of dirty diapers.

Some mothers feel some sense of postpartum, or "post-party," depression. Like when you plan for a party all month, or all year, then it's over, and you are stuck with fun memories, a messy house, and a sink full of dishes.

"It's natural to have emotional ups and downs," my mom would say. "Let yourself experience all of it, with no judgement. This too shall pass. Try to enjoy the simple moments, with no expectations."

Lesson 2: Surrender.

These challenges can be summarized by a key theme: lack of control.

I couldn't control my schedule, my body, my hormones, my partner, or anyone else. And it became especially evident that I couldn't control this baby. When he was hungry, I fed him. When he needed a diaper, I changed him. When he cried, I tried to figure out what was wrong. Whenever I thought I had a moment to breathe, there was something new to which to respond.

So what were my options? I could be stressed and frustrated all the time, or I could shift my perspective. Rather than trying to control something (or someone) over which I had no control, I decided to surrender.

But not to surrender as if giving up. No. *Surrendering attachment to outcome.* Since I prefer to be a relatively structured parent, I tried to focus on process rather than result. When my mood was attached to the "success" of my plan, I often felt frustrated and defeated—so I learned instead to *make a plan, then adapt.*

For example, when I was trying to get my baby on a feeding schedule, rather than being frustrated that he wasn't hungry exactly when I "planned" for him to be hungry, I tried to remember that he wasn't a machine. Just because it didn't work the way I wanted on that occasion, I still got a "gold star" for trying; and I would try again the next time.

With that said, some habits last a lifetime, and others are consistently shifting—especially in the first year of life. It's important to remember that something particularly hard (or easy) right now will likely change. Try to stay away from saying things like "my baby *always* ..." When we relinquish expectations, everything gets easier.

Another "surrender" I found to be effective was to stop trying to control my husband (or any caretaker). When I stopped *expecting daddy to be mommy*, I realized it was more important that he be my teammate than my clone. It became evident that the more I tried to control him, the more frustrated we both became, for when we try to control others, we often create distance rather than closeness.

I embraced the fact that my kids get something different from their father than they do from me. They have a different relationship, and this is vital. I focused on empowering him to be the best parent *he* could be, rather than forcing him to be *me*.

Remember

1. Your life will be altered.
   A. Your sense of accomplishment may be different.
   B. You are in transition.
2. Surrender.
   A. Surrender attachment to outcome.
   B. Focus on process rather than result.
   C. Make a plan, then adapt.
   D. Your baby is not a machine.
      - Consistency is important, but don't expect your little one to be tired or hungry at the exact same moment every day.
      - The moment you think a new habit is formed, something will inevitably change.
   E. Your partner is not you.
      - When you try to control others, you often create distance. rather than closeness.
      - Empower your partner to be the best parent they can be, rather than to be you.

CHAPTER 2

Think for Yourself

Information overload is overwhelming.
Focus on your family.

Lesson 1: What works for some does not work for all.

Because I birthed my babies in my bathtub at home, "You're crazy!" was the usual response I received, along with, "Is that safe? I don't think that's a good idea. What if something goes wrong?"

These are all valid questions. And, understandably, they are the same questions I asked when making the decision to have unmedicated home births with a midwife. When I shared my birth plan with my mom, she didn't respond the way everyone else did. "Tell me more," was all she said.

My mother implicitly trusted me; she trusted my judgment. She wanted to understand. She educated herself. She watched all the videos I recommended and read all the information and research I shared with her. Why? Because she had helped me learn to think for myself; she had taught me that just because there is a "standard" way of doing things, it doesn't mean that is the best way for everyone.

Whether it's how you give birth, whether or not to breastfeed, if you sleep train your baby or co-sleep, you must uncover what is right for *you*, and for your family. *Things are done differently across time and cultures.* It is important to remember, just because it might be "in" right now to swaddle babies, or to put them on a certain schedule, it doesn't mean this technique will stay in fashion forever.

There are countless opposing theories and parenting strategies available. Whether I am looking up something online, asking a friend for advice, or simply listening within, I try to remember that everything is subjective. *Just because it makes sense for someone else doesn't mean it makes sense for me.* As long as your baby is safe and loved, choose whatever path works for your family, even if no one else is doing it!

For example, I didn't want to let my son "cry it out." It seemed horrific. Then after five months of not sleeping more than four hours straight per night, I was at my wits end. When my mom told me that she let me "cry it out" as a baby, I found comfort in knowing that I was a great sleeper, and didn't have any obvious issues as a result, so my husband and I decided to take that route as well.

To be honest, it was the hardest experience I had ever endured. While my son cried, I would sit outside his room crying and writing emails to his "future adult self" about how terrible I felt. Everyone said that the "cry it out" method would work after a few days, but for us, it took many months.

The process was tremendously hard to stick with, but I really believed that, in the grand scheme of things, the sleep training was a minimal amount of struggle in order to prepare my child for a lifetime of positive sleep habits.

This scenario, just like many parenting decisions, is really quite challenging. I dance between short-term versus long-term benefits, deciding when to be flexible or steadfast. These choices, like many others, don't always have clear paths or outcomes, and it is easy to doubt yourself when there are so many competing opinions and perspectives.

Certainly, doing anything for the first time can create feelings of insecurity. It can lead to comparisons and self-criticism. I remember feeling confused when I first became a mom. I had considered myself a confident person, but when my mother-in-law questioned my decision to let my child cry at bedtime, I could feel the tears well up in my eyes as I wanted to scream, "I DON'T KNOW WHAT ELSE TO DO!"

But over time I became better at accepting that it was *okay not knowing what to do.* I wasn't supposed to know. I had never been a parent before. I was learning. This child was an individual, and our experience was unique to us. We were learning together.

The times I didn't know what to do, I would create a plan and give it a try. I envisioned how I *wanted* it to go, rather than focusing on what could go wrong. When we build a plan around how something *could* be, the chances of it manifesting are far greater. When I envisioned my son's childhood full of peaceful nighttime routines, it helped me stick with my sleep training plan.

As Henry Ford once said, "Whether you think you can, or you think you can't—you're right."

Lesson 2: Be consistent.

With my second child, every time I put her bib on, she ripped it off. Every time I put her hat on when she was out in the sun, she ripped it off. You know what I did? I kept putting them back on. And you know what happened? Eventually, she didn't remove them!

New habits don't form overnight. If we want our day, or a specific process, to go a certain way, it's important to create a plan and then stick with it rather than constantly changing plans. It takes time for people to get used to new things. Resistance often arises when people are presented with a new way of doing something, but when we are consistent, children will learn "this is how we do things in our family."

It is important to honor preferences, but at the same time to influence priorities. For example, if you want your child to eat vegetables but they resist, it is important to approach the situation with the understanding that they *can learn* to eat them.

Humans are supposed to eat food from the earth; don't give up just because your child may not want the food you offer at first. If you believe plant-based eating is something your children need to prioritize in their lives, it is vital to keep offering vegetables until they understand that vegetables are the basis of all meals.

If, after a concerted effort, you aren't getting the results you want, try a different approach or a different food, and stick with that for a while. Just because it didn't work the first time, doesn't mean you can't come back later. For example, if your child rejects broccoli every day for a week, don't give up and say "My kid doesn't like broccoli." Rather, say "He doesn't like broccoli *yet*." Most behaviors can be learned if you stick with them.

More importantly, make each activity *fun*. No one wants to feel forced to do anything. Perhaps you can sing songs while eating vegetables. My son loves when I hold up ten fingers and playfully knock each one down as he eats a vegetable. Sometimes he gets a kick out of it when I pretend to be the voice of his belly and I ask him for a veggie. The belly's voice cheers and celebrates as my son takes each bite. Sometimes, I even try reverse psychology and playfully tell him he can't have the veggies. Another option is to draw pictures that explain the importance of eating healthy foods (or going to bed, or not hitting, or whatever task you are trying to accomplish).

If none of your fun and silly efforts work and your child isn't listening to reason, you can lovingly make consequences. "It's okay if you don't eat vegetables, but your body is so sad that_____."

Remember, above all, a power struggle is not helpful in the long run; and be sure to remain *patient* while being consistent.

Lesson 3: Determine your non-negotiables.

What does it take to keep your family sane? What are the priorities and values that are most important? What systems do you need to have in place to keep you and your partner healthy and happy?

When you are clear on your non-negotiables, you can make them the foundation of your home. When children are young, you are basically in survival mode. With my small kids, the non-negotiables are food and sleep. We believe that if our bodies are well-nourished and well-rested then everything else will be easier. We prioritize balanced meals, an unprocessed, plant-based diet, and consistent sleep patterns. In our family, this sets the tone for happier kids, which makes being with our kids much more enjoyable!

Priorities evolve as children grow. Another non-negotiable in my home is that being "mean" is not tolerated. If someone is upset, they are encouraged to express themselves in a healthy manner. I teach my children that it is okay to feel upset, and then we practice taking deep breaths and using words to express ourselves rather than raising our voices or getting aggressive.

If the feelings are too intense to decelerate, it is okay to take a break—but it is never okay to hit or use mean language or tone of voice.

Kids learn the boundaries if you make them clear and are *modeling them yourself.* If you want your children to be calm and respectful, you must be calm and respectful. If you want your children to be polite, don't bark orders at them, be polite in your requests. If you waver and respond differently to the same scenario, a child isn't going to know what to expect from you. In turn, you won't know what to expect from them either!

It's also important to determine your personal and relationship needs. What is a non-negotiable for you? Perhaps you know that you can't function optimally with less than a certain amount of sleep or a certain amount of exercise. What is a non-negotiable for your relationship with your partner? Perhaps you need a consistent date night, or time set aside for talking or intimacy.

A non-negotiable in my marriage is quality time. We have made a point to have quality time together each week. Whether it's committing to be intimate on a regular basis or just taking time to chat at the end of the day, we prioritize our connection to one another.

Just as weight gain can creep up on a body, disconnect can slowly build in a partnership. Forgetting to prioritize the relationship can be a slippery slope in any family. Just as your little ones need a lot of attention, so does your relationship. A strong partnership is the foundation of a healthy home, and the sooner you take your relationship off autopilot, the better it will be.

Prioritizing these non-negotiables can't happen alone. Our society often forgets that it takes a village to raise a child. It is important to ask for help. Asking for help doesn't mean that we *can't* handle it—it means we've set boundaries as to how much we have *chosen* to handle. I know that if I want to be a positive, patient, and kind mother, I need to make sure my needs are met. When I am exhausted or spread too thin, I don't have the inner strength to be patient or kind.

Getting help doesn't have to necessarily mean enlisting grandparents or paid caretakers, there are always options when we think outside the box. You can join a gym that has built-in childcare, or take turns having date nights with your neighbor. The chances of getting the support you need are far greater if you ask for help than if you don't!

Remember

1. What works for some does not work for all.
   A. Things are done differently across time and cultures.
   B. It's okay not knowing; you are learning.
2. Be consistent.
   A. New habits don't form overnight.
      - It's better to try one path consistently rather than switch methods regularly.
      - Make it fun!
      - If after a concerted effort you aren't getting the results you want, try something else and tick with that for a while; you can always return to an earlier strategy in the future.
3. Determine your non-negotiables.
   A. What does it take to keep your family sane?
      - Which priorities are the foundation of your home?
        - Determine your priorities for your kids.
        - Determine your priorities for yourself and partner.
          ~ Ask for help!

CHAPTER 3

Listen

Just because you think you understand, doesn't mean you do.

Lesson 1: Pay attention.

My second child, my daughter, barely cried throughout infancy (unlike my fussier first). Perhaps it was personality, perhaps it was less gas, or perhaps I was a more experienced parent. I guess we will never know for sure, but I remember various moments when she would cry and, instead of reacting to her physical needs, I just lovingly looked her straight in the eyes and let her know she was okay. I remember the first time I did it, I was in disbelief when she stopped crying! She simply stared back at me as if saying, "Thank you for seeing me. I love you, too."

Obviously, this strategy won't always work, but something I did learn about babies is that when their needs are understood and met, they have little reason to fuss. Yet one of the most challenging parts of having a baby is that they can't communicate verbally. In the beginning, there is a lot of guessing until we learn the cues of our child.

As a new mom, I was introduced to a powerful tool called *Dunstan's Baby Language* that changed my world. In this book, author Priscilla Dunstan shares her understanding of the physiological sounds that babies make depending on their physical needs—when you can understand the sounds, you can understand what the baby needs. I recommend watching her interview with Oprah to learn more details of how to read these cues and sounds:

"Owh" – Tired
"Heh" – Discomfort
"Eh"- Burp
"Neh" – Hungry
"Eairh" – Gas

Essentially, when you can decipher the physiological sounds of your baby, you can address their needs before they turn to tears. If your baby needs to burp, you'll know it, so you can quickly offer back pats until it comes out rather than trying to feed them. It was monumental for me to realize that not every cry meant more milk! This understanding changed my world with my son, and by using this technique with my daughter right from the start I barely ever heard her cry.

Avoid power struggles. We know we are really listening when the other person feels heard. If the other person is left frustrated, we can be sure they don't feel understood. As your child gets older, power struggles can become commonplace. It is easy to get frustrated with a child's unreasonable preferences, and to feel the need to remind them that they aren't in charge. However, this is generally not helpful. We don't have to prove we are the boss. If a child feels respected, they will be respectful. If a child feels they have no control, they will do what it takes to gain some.

With small children who have minimal verbal skills, there is a lot of opportunity for frustration (and temper tantrums) when they don't feel understood. Although it does take a bit more strategy and patience, there will be much less resistance when a child feels heard.

For example, whenever I try to tell my toddler son what to do, guess what his response is? You got it. "No!" So where does that leave me? I must be strategic—while also listening to what he wants. "Oh, so you don't want to put on your shirt? I understand. It feels better without it. Maybe I should put it on?" As I pretend to put the shirt over my head, I often get a giggle and a request to give it back.

Rather than dealing with a power struggle every time I want my son to do something, I find ways to give him the control he so desperately desires. I hear him and acknowledge his desires before attempting to address my preference. It takes more thought, it takes more energy, and it can often be exhausting, but it makes life more playful and less oppositional, which to me, feels worth it in the long run. For example, I know that at bedtime my son is going to resist, so rather than force him, I prepare him. I give him five-minute warnings and ask him what the last thing is that he wants to do before bed. I don't make going to bed an option, but everything that happens before bedtime is up to him.

Address the source, not the symptom. In addition to directly listening to a request, also pay attention to what is unspoken. Read between the lines and acknowledge deeper themes. Have compassion for what your children are feeling, respect their perspectives, and be willing to negotiate most things. Don't use threats or fear-tactics to get them to do the right thing. Be patient and strategic. For example, even if you are frustrated that your kids don't want to sleep, respect the fact that it is uncomfortable and scary to be alone in bed. Rather than focusing on your frustration with their disobedience, focus on the source of their upset. Look for solutions to help them deal with their fears—such as teaching them to meditate; talking to them through a child monitoring camera when you leave the room; playing music; letting them read books or play until they are more tired.

Use positive reinforcement and empowerment to get them to *want* to do what is best. Foster a teammate dynamic in your home. Even though they know you have the final say, the hope is that they feel you are fair and that their opinions matter.

Lesson 2: Listen more. Talk less.

I suppose it makes sense that I became a therapist because the practice of "active listening" was the foundation of my upbringing. Therapists are trained to be active listeners—fully present, non-judgmental, and lovingly curious—so they can truly understand another person's experience.

A basic premise of therapy is that when someone feels understood and accepted by another, they can better understand and accept themselves. This self-acceptance creates self-confidence, therefore active listening is fundamental for all mothers.

Here are a few strategies to help you become an active listener:

1. Be "lovingly curious."
   - A. *Try to understand another's perspective.* Most people "listen" while thinking of what they will say next, focusing on their own perspective. Instead, think of the other person in a separate bubble from yourself and try to join them in that bubble to fully understand their viewpoint and experience.
   - B. *Be on the same team.* Make sure your interest in understanding is so you can achieve a shared goal, not win a discussion.

2. Demonstrate you are listening.
   A. *Give body and verbal cues that you are paying attention.* Use eye contact, nod, and say "uh-huh" and "tell me more" to help a person feel connected.
   B. *Clarify what you heard.* Make statements or ask questions to be sure that you understood correctly.
      - "Do you mean that ...?" or "I'm hearing you say ..."
      - "I'm not sure what you mean when you say ..."
   C. *Avoid these words:*
      - "Why"
         - A question starting with "Why" can make someone feel defensive. For example, "Why did you do that?" or "Why do you feel that way?" can elicit feelings of being judged.
         - Instead say "Is there a particular reason you did that?" or "What is making you feel that way?" The intention is to use softer language based on true desire to understand, rather than to prove their perspective wrong.
      - "But"
         - Any time you put the word "but" in a sentence it automatically discards the first part of the sentence. For example, "I hear you are feeling very frustrated, but ..." The focus turns toward whatever is being proven in the second part of the sentence, rather than truly acknowledging the first.
         - Instead, say "and," for example: "I hear you are very frustrated and ..."

- ✦ "Should"
  - Refrain from statements like "You should do this" or "You should or shouldn't have" or "What should you have ...?"
  - Telling someone what they should or shouldn't do makes them feel bossed around. It is an ego-based statement that makes people feel defensive, not open.
  - Instead use "could"
    - ~ Present: Lovingly request "Could you please ..." or suggest "you could ..."
    - ~ Past: If an interaction already happened, you can ask "What *could* have been done differently?" Use it as an opportunity to reflect together and think about other options that might be used in the future, rather than working from a "right/wrong" standpoint.

3. Repeat what you heard in your own words.
   A. *Summarize content.* "I'm hearing you say that ..." or "It sounds like ..."
   B. *Identify and empathize with feelings.* "That must have made you feel ..." or "You must feel so ..."

Learning to be an active listener is like learning an invaluable new language, for effective communication is the foundation of good relationships. When your children (or partner) feel understood and accepted, they feel loved and connected.

Lesson 3: When you care, people share.

My mom always said that parenting just kept getting better. She said she preferred us when we could talk and share with her over the baby stage. As we grew up, she was interested in really *knowing* us. "I already know what *I* think about it, I'm more interested to know what *you* think about it." This was a common theme in the way my mom approached conversations.

Just because we have our own opinions, doesn't mean other people's opinions aren't equally valid. When we care, we want to know what the *other person* is experiencing. Be open to learning. Don't assume you understand. Ask questions. Avoid being condescending; or trying to be right in order to make the other person wrong. Be curious about the details and empathize with what the other person is feeling. Encourage them to think for themselves and trust that it is best if they find their own answers. When you connect with people (in their "bubble") they will feel connected to you.

Remember

1. Pay attention.
   - A. Research *Dunstan's Baby Language*.
   - B. Avoid power struggles.
   - C. Address the source, not the symptoms.

2. Listen more. Talk less.
   - A. Be an active listener.
   - B. Be "lovingly curious."
     - ✦ Try to understand their perspective.
     - ✦ Be on the same team.
   - C. Demonstrate you are listening.
     - ✦ Give body and verbal cues that you are paying attention.
     - ✦ Clarify what you heard.
       - • "Do you mean that …?"
       - • "I'm not sure what you mean when you say …?"
         - ~ Don't say "WHY?"
         - ~ Don't say "BUT"
         - ~ Don't say "SHOULD"
   - D. Repeat what you heard in your own words.
     - ✦ Summarize content.
     - ✦ Identify and empathize with feelings.

3. When you care, people share.

CHAPTER 4

Decrease Drama

Create a peaceful environment.
Enjoy peaceful children.

Lesson 1: Set the intention to create a drama-free environment.

"Does your mom ever get mad?" My friends would often ask when I was growing up. My answer was usually, "Not really."

How was this possible? Well, for starters, my mom took really good care of her physical and emotional health, so she didn't have a lot of pent-up frustrations to take out on us. In addition to active listening and self-care, my parents highly valued a peaceful and drama-free environment. They didn't see any benefit to yelling or being critical. They believed that positive reinforcement and loving support were the foundation for raising good, balanced children. They focused on the bigger picture. If we were healthy and safe, everything else could be figured out.

Consequently, they had an exceptionally wide range for what they considered acceptable. If we stayed within these wide boundaries, nothing was especially wrong. This helped them to stay calm. As a result, they didn't say "no" very often either.

Use "no" intentionally. Some parents feel like they are saying "no" all day long. Rather than responding with a negative, it is helpful to try to say "okay" to most requests:

- "Okay, let me think about it.
- "Okay, we can do that later."
- "Okay, after you do x we can do that for five minutes. I'll put on the timer."

When children feel they are getting what they want, they will be less likely to battle for power.

And instead of saying no, you can also say things like:

- "I hear you want *x*, and yet I want y, so what should we do about this?"
- "Yes, we can xyz [another time] after we do [desired behavior]."
- "Yes, and ..."

Set the intention to flow *with* them, instead of *against* them. The words "no" or "don't" can often foster a feeling of rejection that can automatically create opposition. It is important to remember that their energy is malleable, and it is affected by your energy. Think of yourself as the leader of the energy in your home; try to flow with their energy into the outcome you desire rather than attempting to force it. If you approach a situation with patience and ease, your energy and your strategic communication can often assist them in coming to your desired conclusion on their own.

Because my parents didn't say "no" very often, when they did, we generally listened. For example, voices were never raised for simple annoyances, so since we weren't accustomed to being yelled at, if we ran into the street and heard a strong reaction, we listened.

The word *no* can certainly be used when something is significant, as a delineation of clear boundaries, of what is acceptable or not.

"No, you cannot hit your sister" is different than "No, you can't wear that striped shirt with your pajama pants to school."

Lesson 2: Be self-reflective.

When you want to tone down the drama, there are a few fundamental self-reflection strategies I recommend:

Give what you want to get. If you want your kids to be better listeners, you must become a better listener. If you want them to be more affectionate, you need to be more affectionate, and so on. This goes for all relationships. Focus on what you can *give*, rather than what you want to receive. When we model the behavior we want to receive, we are more likely to get it in return.

Be aware of your inner anxiety scale. Think of your level of anxiety on a scale from one to ten. One is blissful, and ten is ready to jump off the Brooklyn Bridge. When you are anywhere above a five or six, it is very likely that little things can push you over the edge. For example, when your kid doesn't want to brush their teeth and you are late for school, if your level of anxiety is at a three, then maybe this frustrating moment pushes you up to a four or five. Yet, if you are starting at a six, this simple situation can suddenly push you to a seven or an eight, and you may find yourself getting angry and loud over something insignificant.

Shift energy from hard to soft. When we feel angry, it's important to look at what is going on inside. For example, anger is usually hiding vulnerability; when we feel helpless, or out of control, we can feel weak. Since anger is a response that helps us feel strong in a moment of weakness, one way to address this is to take a deep breath and step away from the situation. Then, when you take that deep belly breath, you can ask yourself "What is really going on here? What is my more vulnerable feeling?"

Acknowledging the more vulnerable feeling changes your energy from hard to soft. It can also make you feel more grounded and surrendered in the moment, as well as help you to be more connected to yourself and those around you. Soft doesn't mean to give in; soft simply suggests being *open*, or not guarded. Rather than yelling and trying to force your child to follow your instructions, you can say "I need your help. I'm feeling very overwhelmed right now."

Being tender is a form of true mental strength, not weakness. You can have soft energy, yet strong (clear and direct) requests.

Another trick to shifting energy from hard to soft is to use *vulnerable, loving statements*. Softening statements can also help you to put down your ego and be more open:

I'm sorry.

Please forgive me.

Thank you.

I love you.

If you can't get yourself to say them aloud to another person, practice saying them to yourself, or to the Divine, as often as possible. Once you start softening on the inside, it will likely be easier to do so on the outside.

Don't take your frustrations out on your children. It's important that your child doesn't feel as if they are an inconvenience. While it is natural, and not unexpected, for parents to sometimes become stressed or frustrated, do your best to calmly express any frustration that arises—and always take personal responsibility for having those feelings. If you have too much on your plate, adjust your circumstances whenever possible, getting the support you might need so that your kids don't receive the brunt of your discontent.

I know when I have too much of an agenda everything is harder because I am impatient and expect too much of my children. When they aren't on my timeline, everything they do feels annoying to me because it's not what I want. To stay calm, I try to plan ahead, remembering that everything takes longer than expected, and that it's not *their* responsibility when things don't go the way I planned.

Lesson 3: Be grateful.

Life is full of challenges and difficulties. There is no doubt about that. This will not end, for it is a part of the human experience. However, one way to approach challenges with more ease is to see them as opportunities for growth. Instead of complaining and focusing on your frustration, it's helpful to consider what you could be learning from a challenge, and the ways in which you will grow. When we accept what is, we can rewire our brains to embrace challenges in order to become *learners*, rather than *complainers*.

When we take that moment to breathe, we can give ourselves an opportunity to *see the big picture*. And when we keep life in perspective, it's easier to realize that very few of the daily occurrences we experience are actually a big deal. This makes it easier to be grateful. Taking a moment to realize how good your life is relative to the horrific circumstances that exist elsewhere will really help to keep the drama in check. It may be disturbing, but I am often very aware that in this moment there are people somewhere in the world who are being violently tortured, molested, even murdered. Others are starving, sick, suffering from pain or the loss of loved ones, and simply trying to survive.

From my travels I have very real images of the many people throughout the world who lack running water, hygiene, and freedom. I know that regardless of what happens in my life—even the tragic loss of my precious mother—I still have more to be grateful for than not. I believe gratitude is truly the most empowering frame of mind. When we are grateful, life is less dramatic, and fewer things are "a big deal," which makes everything easier. Remember: *It could always be worse.*

Here are a few simple statements to help find gratitude and access a bigger perspective:

Say "So what?" So what if we are late to school? So what if his clothes don't match? When we look at the worst-case scenario of most situations, we start to realize that most of them are trivial.

Replace a peevish thought with "At least ..." and then find something for which to be grateful. At least we have running water. At least no one is sick right now. When we remember to take a moment to reflect, we can become aware of how it can always be worse, and that there is much to appreciate in any current scenario. For example: "My mom died instantly in a car accident—at least she didn't suffer. At least I didn't have to see her lifeless body. At least nothing was left unsaid. At least it wasn't both my parents, or more of my family."

Instead of "I have to ..." say "I get to ..." I get to clean these dishes because I am able-bodied and have a home. I get to deal with my child's tantrum because I have a healthy child who has opinions. I get to be exhausted at the end of the day because I have a beautiful family and a full life. This simple switch helps you realize that complaints common to you are actually blessings to many other people.

In addition to the statements you can say to yourself, these are a few beliefs that are important to consider:

When someone is hardest to love is when they need love the most. This was one of my mom's favorite sayings. Tantrums, aggression, negativity—basically any frustrating behavior—is usually evidence of something deeper that needs to be addressed. As mentioned, our anger is a guard for our more vulnerable feelings, therefore the negative feelings or behaviors of others highlight their own deeper discomfort. It is important to read between the lines and to look beyond the behavior. *Treat the source, not the symptom.*

It's better to be loving than to be right. Humility is a virtue. I remember as a teenager when I was short and snappy with my mom, rather than being aggressive or offended in return, she would *assume the best in me.* She assumed that something was going on with me that made me less patient or kind. She would make it clear that *it was okay not to be okay*, and that she was there for me if I needed a hug.

Hugs trump logic. When you approach your child's aggression with frustration, it adds fuel to the fire. Yet sometimes we try to be logical and reason with their emotions, and it doesn't help either. Regardless of the age, but particularly with small children, when emotions are raging, a hug helps shift energy from hard to soft. It helps access the tears and more vulnerable feelings that are guarded by aggression.

When in doubt, hugs will always provide an excellent remedy!

Remember

1. Set the intention for a peaceful, drama-free environment.
   A. Use "no" intentionally and sparingly.

2. Be self-reflective.
   A. Give what you want to receive.
      - ✦ If you want others to listen better, you need to listen better, etc.

   B. Be aware of your inner anxiety scale (1-10).
   C. Shift energy from hard to soft.
      - ✦ Tenderness is not weakness.
      - ✦ Acknowledge your vulnerable feelings, such as helplessness, when feeling angry or frustrated.
      - ✦ Step away from challenging situations and take deep breaths.
      - ✦ Say softening statements to yourself or someone else:
        - I'm sorry.
        - Please forgive me.
        - Thank you.
        - I love you.

   D. Don't take your frustrations out on your children.
      - ✦ Make sure your children don't feel like an inconvenience.

3. Be grateful.
   A. Be a learner, not a complainer.
   B. See the big picture. Remember, it could always be worse.
      - Ask yourself "so what?" and get okay with the worst-case scenario.
      - Start with "At least ..." and find something for which to be grateful.
      - Say "I *get* to" instead of "I *have* to."
   C. Beliefs that help us feel grateful.
      - When a child is hardest to love is when they need love the most.
         - Treat the source, not the symptom.
      - It's better to be loving than to be right.
         - Assume the best in your children.
         - It's okay not to be okay.
      - Hugs trump logic.

CHAPTER 5

Put Down Your Phone

Your phone will always be small,
your kids won't. Be a present parent.

Lesson 1: Our kids need our attention.

Whenever my husband is on a screen, I am quick to remind him to put it down. I notice when the kids are trying to get his attention, and how frustrated they are by his distracted responses to them. I feel bad that the screen seems to be more significant to him than they are in the moment. Sometimes we even get into a tiff about it.

Then I have my moments when he's the one telling *me*, and I'm humbled to realize I do the exact same thing! When I'm staring at my own screen, I am so consumed with what I'm doing that I have no idea how my kids are feeling in response to being ignored.

When I was a kid, parents didn't have the distraction of cell phones, but at this point, it's hard to imagine life without them. We have yet to discover the outcome of a generation whose parents are constantly staring at screens, and I don't think I'm going out on a limb in saying the results will probably not be so great.

Our monkey minds are constantly thinking of random things, and we literally have every answer to every question at our fingertips. It's amazing technology—yet completely disconnecting. Our kids don't know if we are checking the weather or the time, all they know is that our eyes are on our phone and not on them. Just because we are with them, doesn't mean we are present to them. *Our kids need our authentic attention.*

As an effort to be more present with my children, I use phone features to filter calls and keep it silent when I don't want to be distracted. In this way, I can make time to give my kids my undivided attention—like my mom gave to me.

Lesson 2: Create quality, undistracted time with your kids.

When it comes to parenting, it's easy to just go through the motions, trying to get everything done, so that we can get the kids to sleep and finally relax! But how often do we have time with our kids with no agenda? In our busy lives it can feel like we are being unproductive if we are simply doing nothing. However, when we make it a point to create *quality, undistracted time with our kids*, they get to experience *our undivided attention.*

I know that after a while it can get a bit monotonous to read the same children's book over and over; and how long can we really shake the rattle before our minds wander off? Even today, while playing with my son, I started clipping his nails amidst doing a puzzle. It's hard not to get distracted. However, there is little that is more important than spending quality time with our children, which is why "do nothing time" or "play time" are great items to plan into our schedule.

This is not to suggest we must stop our life and not work or get other things done. However, it does mean that when it's time to be with our children, we try to really *be* with them, and when we need to do other things, we clarify that it's time to be apart. And if you can be out of their sight when you are being productive, that's even better—this way they won't try to get your attention when it's not available.

Lesson 3: Encourage "boredom."

I notice that my kids want to look at screens much more when I am looking at my screen. But when we all put down our screens, we open ourselves up to *boredom*. And, most importantly, by doing so *we invite creativity, connection, and imagination.*

I too start to think outside the box when we are bored, and find myself coming up with imaginative games or discovering toys that were buried in the closet. When we have "nothing to do," we receive the gift of having to figure out something to do in that moment.

It is *very* important to minimize screen time for children. When they don't get the instant gratification of entertainment, they learn to deal with the discomfort of boredom and become empowered enough to use their imagination.

When we do give our children screens however, it's important to regulate what they watch. Rather than handing them a device and letting them skip from one show to the next, it's better for the development of their attention span to focus on one slow-paced show until the end. Choose a show or series that teaches them something. Whether it's reading, math, science, or Spanish, I gain comfort in knowing that my kids are getting smarter when watching, instead of zoning out on something mindless. One show that I highly recommend above all others is *Daniel Tiger's Neighborhood*—a cartoon developed as a spin-off from *Mister Roger's Neighborhood* about a four-year old boy tiger and his family. Through simple stories and songs, it teaches healthy approaches to handle challenging feelings while also teaching emotional intelligence. What's even better is, when I watch, I learn new parenting skills too! For example, how to handle issues with sharing, going to sleep, brushing teeth, trying new food, etc.

Lesson 4: Kids who get attention are less likely to act out for attention.

My mom always made a point of being present with us. I never felt that anything was more important to her than me. I always felt a hug, or a kiss, took precedence over anything else in the world. It made me feel seen, heard, and loved. As a result, I felt connected and didn't act out to get her attention.

Children feel their level of priority from our attention. "Look at me!" can arise in many forms. Kids often act on impulse, so yelling, hitting, kicking, etc., are usually red flags that they need attention. Rather than getting frustrated with my son's tantrums, I try to respond with "Do you need attention?" Surprisingly, he is often quieted as he nods humbly in response. I then explain that he can ask me for my attention, and he doesn't ever need to act unkindly; "Mom, I need attention" is always sufficient.

And when he asks directly for attention I try to address his request promptly, most often providing him with the attention he has requested. If it's not appropriate timing I explain why, and then request that he be patient, letting him know when he can expect my attention once more.

In addition to addressing the undesirable behavior, it's also helpful to praise both desired behavior and direct requests. Acknowledgment and praise for appropriate behavior can be great ways to get our kids to do more of it!

Remember

1. Your kids need your *authentic* attention.
2. Make quality, undistracted time with your kids.
3. Encourage "boredom."
   - Technology-free time can elicit connection, creativity, and imagination.
4. Kids who get attention are less likely to act out for attention.
   - When a child acts out, it's a red flag that they need your attention.
   - Acknowledge and praise desired behavior to encourage more of it.

CHAPTER 6

Make Memories

Do something different. Interesting experiences make interesting people.

Lesson 1: Do something different.

My mom loved to travel. When I say travel, I mean *travel*, not just vacation. She wanted to see, feel, taste, hear, and fully experience life. Ever since my brother and I were young, my mom and dad exposed us to the world outside our little "love bubble." During the summers we would go away as a family. We would stay in places with no hot water, sleep in the jungle with local people, go on bamboo rafts, ride on elephants, camels, or donkeys, hike, take overnight trains in foreign lands, explore cities, see landscapes, meet strangers—you name it, we've done it.

Travel like this has given me some of my most special and vivid memories. When we traveled, we were open to experiencing life in a whole different way. Everything that happened was an opportunity for adventure. Every person we met was an opportunity for connection. My mom would wander to villagers' homes and end up "chatting" with wrinkly, toothless women who didn't speak any of the four languages she spoke. They would hug and giggle as if they were old girlfriends.

Random, quirky memories such as this give me great satisfaction in knowing that *she truly lived.*

For my mom, it was travel; for you, it could be something else. What are the different experiences that make you feel present, connected, and alive? *How can you do more of it?*

Lesson 2: Make simple moments special. Be wise enough to be silly. Have fun!

Recently I've been extra excited about working on this book which has, in some ways, made writing about parenting seem more fun than playing with my kids—in fact, I've found it harder to be present because my mind is spinning with all the things I want to be sure to remember to include. How ironic that writing this book is keeping me from doing the very things I'm advocating!

Then I had a revelation: I need to figure out how to make playing with them more fun *for me*. I remembered a time when I was lazily chasing my kids on the playground, waiting for the minutes to pass, and then making the decision to switch gears and play full-out. I started dodging the kids on the playground, and really trying not to be caught. I had so much fun! I felt alive, connected, and even proud. It was the same sort of satisfaction I get from accomplishing a goal or being productive with my work. I realized that being fully engaged and having fun with my kids is an achievement in and of itself.

In addition to making moments fun by shifting the mindset, my mom also found ways to make our *simple life experiences special.* She never let life get in the way of living. And we didn't have to have some big, extravagant experience to have a good time. Money or other excuses never kept her from doing random, fun, memorable things.

Here are a few examples of simple moments to which she added a special twist:

- Whenever she would see me, whether first thing in the morning or when I got home from school, she greeted me with a smile, a hug, and a kiss.
- Instead of just watching a movie at home, she would make us ticket stubs and popcorn and we would play "movie theater."
- When we couldn't go outside, we made secret forts in the living room from chairs and blankets and invited the stuffed animals over as guests.
- My lunch at school was packed with a love note on a napkin.
- I was woken up gently with a sweet and silly good morning song.
- In high school, when I had friends over, she would bring us cookies. My friends thought she was cool, and she got to see what we were up to behind the closed door!
- When she picked me up at the airport after being away, I would see her from a distance jumping up and down with excitement to welcome me back. Then I would arrive at the house to be greeted with "welcome home" posters.
- She once hired a man to take us on a handmade gondola ride when we had visitors from out of town. (They got welcome posters too!)
- When we had picnics on the beach, she made sparkling cider towers out of plastic champagne glasses—that always fell when she started to pour the cider!
- When my son turned two months old, I received a video of her and my dad wearing silly hats and holding stuffed animals, singing, "Happy second birth month to you!"

Lesson 3: Focus on experience over achievement.

In addition to creating silly, special, and sweet moments in our daily lives, my mom paid attention to what interested us. She encouraged us to lean into our curiosities, even if it wasn't convenient for her. If she didn't care about a topic that peaked our interest, she would *learn to care* about it.

She believed that living a full, interesting, and connected life was the truest accomplishment. It didn't matter if we were *successful*—she cared that we felt fulfilled. It didn't matter if we won the sports game, she cared that we enjoyed playing. It didn't matter if we got straight A's, she just wanted to know that we had tried our best. Her focus was always on *experience over achievement*.

She trusted that through experiencing life we would learn, grow, and evolve. She understood that pressure to achieve can interfere with the enjoyment of an experience. She also understood that the path to achievement is full of enriching experiences.

Here are some examples of ways that she embraced our curiosities and encouraged us to more fully experience our passions:

- When my pet parakeets started breeding, she got me bigger cages. She saw my interest in animals and decided it was valuable to learn about nature, life, death, responsibility, and cleanliness. I ended up with an aviary of thirty-four parakeets in my bedroom! To her, it was worth the challenge of finding a pet sitter when we traveled because of the priceless experiences I had with my feathered friends.
- At a circus performance I told her I wanted to be a performer, so after the show she took me up to the ring leader to find out how I could join the circus. Guess what? The next season, my eight-year-old self did! I went to circus practice every day after school even though it ended at nine at night.

- When we went fishing and brought a fish home for dinner, my ten-year-old self decided that I no longer wanted to eat animals, even though my favorite foods were steak and ribs. Guess what? She understood. If I got the protein I needed, she was willing to learn how to cook vegetarian food. (This lasted eight years!)
- My little brother really liked baseball cards and autographs, so what did my parents do on the weekends? Take him to games, of course. They would not only stay after the game to meet the players, but they sometimes followed a team's bus to the players' hotel after a game (not knowing where it was going—even on school nights!) They would go as far as bringing pictures of my brother taken with the players from the previous season for the athletes to sign.
- When my brother joined his school's cross-country team, my parents supported him in organizing a run across the state of Florida to raise funds for people with disabilities. And when he wanted to run a marathon, guess who cheered him on? My sixteen-year-old brother ran that marathon faster than everyone in his age division.
- When my brother wanted to get more involved in high school, my mom encouraged him to start the organization that he had been talking about, which would bring high school kids to underdeveloped countries in order to help expose them to the world. My parents didn't hesitate to take a group of teenagers to stay with local families on dirt floor huts in Guatemala, and my brother's organization got so popular that the local press couldn't get enough of it.
- When it came time to apply to college, my mom spent countless nights with my brother putting together a VHS compilation of all his media coverage. Was Harvard the goal? Not necessarily. Was it the result? Yep.

Lesson 4: Connect with others.

There was a seventy-five-year study on what makes a good life—the only study of its kind and duration. They interviewed 724 men over their entire lives. You know what they concluded? People with loving, fulfilling relationships are happier than those without. (For more about this study, watch the *Ted Talk*: "*What Makes a Good Life?* Lessons from the longest study on happiness.")

But my mom didn't need to read the study; she already knew this. She made a point to get out of her own "bubble" and see what was going on in the "bubbles" of her friends and family. She made time for those she loved, and regularly kept in touch with those who were far away. She cared to celebrate their joys and be there for their challenges. She made a point of maintaining relationships with those about whom she cared. Everyone she loved felt it from her actions.

When my beloved mother passed, we basically held a memorial "tour." We hosted three memorial services in three different cities to accommodate all the people whom she loved (and who loved her). We even had an open microphone, so people could share their thoughts, feelings, and stories. What was the common theme? Everyone had a special relationship with my mom, and it was fun to hear the memories and perspectives from people I didn't even know. She went out of her way to do sweet things, send thoughtful gifts, and ask meaningful questions. Although I used to roll my eyes or poke fun at her need to "celebrate" silly moments in life, now that she is gone, we all have so many special memories to cherish.

Remember

1. Do something different.
2. Make simple moments special. Be wise enough to be silly. Have fun!
3. Focus on experience over achievement. (Experience can lead to achievement.)
   - Embrace your children's curiosities.
4. Connect with others.
   - People with loving, fulfilling relationships are happier than those without.
   - When people are at your memorial, how will they remember you?

CHAPTER 7

Cultivate Confidence

We create their belief system.
Brainwash wisely.

Lesson 1: Be intentional.

I had a proud mommy moment the other day when I overheard my son telling my daughter that he loved her, and how it important it is to share and give hugs and kisses. Not only did my heart melt, but I giggled to myself at my masterful brainwashing. Certainly, the moment was short-lived, and whining and grabbing ensued, but witnessing him speak my words as his own was powerful and eye-opening.

As a therapist, I am constantly reminded of how much parents influence their children's belief systems. Children say and do what they hear and see, and since my mother understood this, she very intentionally taught us beliefs that would create a foundation of confidence.

My sister-in-law was sharing a story about my brother recently, and she mentioned how he rarely says anything bad about anyone. Rather than find frustration or fault in people's differences, he says that everyone is "quirky" and that's what makes the world interesting. I loved hearing her say that, not only because it made me love my brother more, but because even though I had never personally used those words, I had the same belief system instilled in me from my mom.

Below are some of the key beliefs with which my mom intentionally "brainwashed" us. Although they are powerful in and of themselves, it is important to know that *children mostly do what we do, rather than what we say*. It was vital in my upbringing that not only did we hear these beliefs in words, but we saw them in action:

"*You can do anything you put your mind to.*" I distinctly remember truly believing this phrase when I got hard contact lenses at age seven and put them in by myself. I remember the fear I felt about sticking this hard, foreign object on my eyeball, and I remember the pride I felt when I successfully did it. Throughout my life, my mom always reminded me of challenging times like this that I overcame by simply deciding that I could.

"*You won't know unless you try.*" Although my brother told me that he didn't want to apply to Harvard University for fear of being rejected, it was due to believing in this statement that he took the plunge. Not only did this belief get him accepted, but it motivated him, a government major, to randomly take a shot at the movie business, which led him to co-produce the highest grossing Sundance Film Festival winner to date at the age of twenty-nine. As much credit as I give my brother for his unbelievable successes, I know that his confidence was fostered by our mom.

"*It doesn't hurt to ask.*" Whether it was an upgrade on the plane or a refund on a terrible meal, my mom knew our chances of getting what we wanted were zero if we weren't willing to directly, respectfully ask. When I first moved to Florida, I was introduced to a woman who organized the largest event for professional women in Miami. At that point, I had very little speaking experience but figured it didn't hurt to ask, so I had my team create a professional proposal for the next event. Not only was I accepted as a speaker, but I was asked to be on the board for the event as well!

"*What's the worst that could happen?*" Fear gets in the way of most success. This question can really help us to get comfortable with our worst-case scenario and make it easier to move forward toward our goals. "So what if they say no? So what if it doesn't work?"

"*Envision it.*" "Get as detailed as you possibly can," she used to say. "Feel it, see it, hear it, believe it, and then let it go into the universe." Visualizing doesn't mean creating expectations; it isn't about creating attachment to the outcome—it is simply about getting energetically aligned with the path that we want to follow. It is also important to realize that it is not possible to manifest something that we aren't clear we really want.

"*There is no such thing as failure, just opportunities to learn.*" If we try something and don't succeed, we just learned something that didn't work. When we aren't scared to fail, it is much easier to proceed—and succeed.

"*Be soft, yet strong.*" As lovey and gooey as my mom was, she was, by no means, a pushover. I distinctly remember witnessing lovingly strong conversations with people with whom she felt disrespected by, taken advantage of, or misunderstood. She managed to maintain soft energy while making clear boundaries as to what was acceptable to her. For example, "I'm sorry, that doesn't work for me." Or "Perhaps I misunderstood your intention, because I expected ..."

My mother cultivated confidence in us because she was confident in herself. She was intentional in the way she spoke to us and knew that she was our role model for how to engage with the world around us.

Remember

1. Be intentional
   - You can do anything you put your mind to.
   - You won't know unless you try.
   - It doesn't hurt to ask.
   - What's the worst that could happen?
   - Envision it.
   - There is no such thing as failure.
   - Be soft yet strong.

CHAPTER 8

Empower Adolescence

Our children will become adults.
Clarify curiosities.

Lesson 1: Share about love, relationships, sex, and safety

I met a boy, or to be exact, a young man. I was fourteen years old, it was summer, and my friend and I were studying and living abroad in a homestay in Mexico. It wasn't conventional to send kids that age to such programs—which was evident, as all the kids in the program were college students. However, my mom thought outside the box. Not only was it a great opportunity to improve my Spanish and immerse myself in a new culture, but it was also a chance for her adolescent daughter to gain more independence and confidence. She wanted me to have some "real world experiences" that one might not get while paddle boarding at summer camp. The best part: I had my first kiss! I can still remember the last night of my trip. I embraced this beautiful man, beneath the flickering streetlight, while the misty drizzle tickled my cheeks. It was magical, just like in *Dirty Dancing*! I had found my Johnny. It was the moment of my dreams.

Prior to this, whenever my friends suggested I make out with a random boy in the closet at a party, I declined. I made it known that I wanted my first kiss to be special. However, it wasn't a surprise that I responded this way. My mom had started teaching me about love, sex, and true intimacy at a really young age. I remember the mind-blowing night in second grade, when she read me and my four-year-old brother an age-appropriate book called *Where Do Babies Come From?*

She realized that we were going to learn about sex at some point, and that rather than avoiding the topic and having us fend for ourselves, it was important to empower us with knowledge and understanding. There was never any fear or shame attached to these concepts. As we grew older, *sex was presented as an opportunity for a beautiful connection* with someone for whom we care deeply, someone who respects and adores us, someone we can talk with openly, and someone who has our best interests at heart.

Even through high school my mom and I often had our most cherished chats before bed. I felt comfortable sharing with her my ups and downs of adolescence because she never preached; she shared. She never judged; she listened. She knew very clearly that *when we tell someone not to do something, it doesn't mean they won't do it—it just means they won't talk to us about it.*

So, when I came back home gushing about my one perfect night with this magical man, this college student, again, my mom listened. She didn't jump to conclusions or make judgments. She wanted to know more. Like any intelligent mother, she was aware of the possibilities. Maybe this guy was a creep. Maybe he was after one thing. Maybe he was a loser who couldn't get girls his own age.

After a year of long distance communication—handwritten letters, AOL instant message chats, pager texts, and extensive nightly long-distance phone calls—it became clear that my one starlit evening with this older gentleman meant something to him too.

Interestingly and conveniently, my mom had a reason to go to the city in which he lived. She was subtle in her protective ways, always looking out for me, but never projected fear or anxiety. She simply wanted to meet this man who had won her daughter's heart.

So she met him. It had been more than a year since our one magical night together. We hadn't even seen each other since then. "Just a fling," many parents would think. But he was important to me, so he became important to her.

Not surprisingly, after a three-hour conversation and a few slices of pizza, they felt a special bond. Over the next few years she helped him orchestrate many surprise visits, and eventually even suggested my sixteen-year-old self join him on his backpacking trip to Europe when he graduated college!

Other mothers thought she was nuts. Perhaps she was. Why was she encouraging her high school daughter to fall more in love with a college man? *Because she knew what was most important.*

Through that relationship, I learned what it felt like to be adored, respected, and understood by an attractive, educated, wise, and kind man (who also happened to be committed to saving my virginity until I was of age). And being in that relationship kept me from wasting my time with disrespectful high school boys and drama.

This transitional time set the tone for future relationships as well. It is no coincidence that both my brother and I created strong, loving marriages with spouses who also come from healthy homes.

The point of the story? My mom taught me about true love, intimacy, and safety—enough that I could manifest it in my own teenage life. She knew that adolescence was a challenging time; that it was hard to develop a strong sense of self amidst all the hormones and peer pressure. She trusted herself. She trusted her ability to parent. She trusted that this relationship was a good one for me, even if it was unconventional. Like almost always, she was right. Much of who I am today, and my future relationships, were influenced by that transformational time in my life.

When I called "Johnny," now a dear friend, to tell him of my mom's passing, he was driving. I made him pull the car over, so I could safely share what had happened. After we shed some tears together, we hung up the phone, and he wiped the fog from the windshield to be on his way. To his shock and amazement, when he looked up he found that he had pulled over in front of the road sign *Betsy Lane*. Sending me the photo was insufficient—although it had been nearly twenty years since we first met in Mexico, this man, who most moms would consider to be *just* a teenage crush, was so affected that he took the next flight to attend her funeral.

Lesson 2: Talk about alcohol, drugs, and safety.

Alcohol. This was something my mom didn't discuss preemptively. Maybe because my parents weren't drinkers, it didn't occur to them that kids might be into it. As a result, my high school self didn't quite know where they stood on the topic. So, I had a few months of devious behavior—drinking in my bedroom at slumber parties with my girlfriends and sneaking out of the house to walk around the neighborhood at night. Nothing too crazy at the time, but it's a slippery slope.

Luckily, I got caught.

I distinctly remember the "talk" I got when they found my stash of wine coolers. Rather than being in trouble, or reprimanded, they used it as an opportunity to find out what was happening. They listened. They wanted to understand what I was doing. They cared to know why I wasn't sharing with them. I don't remember the details of the conversation, but I do remember the outcome.

I was never told that I couldn't drink alcohol. They knew saying that would just push me away; other kids were exploring drugs and alcohol, and my parents couldn't control it. *They felt it was more important to have open lines of communication than to control me.*

I left the conversation feeling grateful for my parents compared to those of my friends. I was comforted in knowing that I could talk to them about alcohol and understood that their deepest concern was for my safety. They told me they would always pick me up if I was drunk, and I would never be in trouble for calling. It was very clear that my life was more important than anything else, and drinking and driving was never okay for me or anyone with whom I was spending time. The result? I decided to stop drinking. I became the designated driver for all my drunken teenage friends. Even in college I never got into drugs or alcohol—I decided it was cool to be the sober girl who could dance on the tables.

Moral of the story? What kids need most is to feel safe, respected, and understood. *When our kids feel trusted and acknowledged, they are empowered to make their own positive decisions.*

Remember

1. Share about love, relationships, sex, and safety.
   A. Focus more on understanding and empathizing than teaching and preaching.
      - *When we tell someone not to do something, it doesn't mean they won't do it. It means they likely won't talk to us about it.*
2. Talk about alcohol, drugs, and safety.
   A. Be lovingly curious, open, and non-judgmental.
      - It is more important to have open communication than to attempt to control.

   B. The goal is for your child to make good decisions because they care about themselves and their wellbeing, not because they are fearful of you or of consequences.

CHAPTER 9

Be on the Same Team

All perspectives matter.
Create teammates, not opponents.

Lesson 1: Challenging people are our teachers.

There are times when I dream about running away. Everyone annoys me. My kids are acting insane. My husband has his own agenda. I think about traveling to foreign lands to feel free from the stress of the daily grind. Most often I simply yearn for a quiet bubble bath!

Getting along with others isn't always easy. Think about how many thoughts and feelings you have in a day. If someone were to track all that goes on within you, it would be a complex chart. Likewise, everyone else has their own inner experience.

To assume that other people think or feel the exact things we do, at the same time, is quite an unrealistic expectation. Considering all that goes on within each of us in each moment, coexistence is an incredible feat!

But beneath our different thoughts, feelings, preferences, and experiences, we are one. I like to think of humans as ice cubes floating in water; we are seemingly separate but of the same essence—*love*.

When someone gets under our skin, it says more about us than it does about them. However, it often feels easier to focus on someone who bothers us than on the true reasons for why we are bothered. When we see relationships as opportunities for self-reflection, *we learn about ourselves through our reactions to people*. If we are making someone else wrong, we are coming from our ego, creating separation instead of unity.

Multiple perspectives can exist simultaneously—more than one person can be "right." This awareness allows us to be more open to understanding, and able to embrace multiple perspectives. A common metaphor that represents this is the story of the five blind men touching different parts of an elephant who all have different ideas about what an elephant is. One may think it is flimsy like the tail, another may think it is long and hose-shaped like the trunk, another may think it is big and hefty like its leg. If they fight to prove each is right, they miss the opportunity to walk around and experience the other perspectives, and realize they are all right!

Through this process of appreciating diverse perspectives, we can also *become more vulnerable and receptive to feedback*. When we accept that multiple perspectives exist, we understand it is natural for others to see us differently than we see ourselves.

My mother's ability to be open in this way made it easy for me to give her feedback. When she did something that bothered me, I felt comfortable sharing because I knew she wouldn't be defensive. She always wanted to learn and grow, so if I had insight that could help her to do so, she willingly received it.

In our home, it was clear that we were on the same team. It was acceptable to have different perspectives, and we were encouraged to listen to and learn from our different viewpoints. As a result, we learned to address all people with this same approach and worked together to find solutions that were acceptable to all.

Remember

1. Challenging people are our teachers.
    - We learn about ourselves through our reactions to other people.
    - Multiple perspectives can exist simultaneously; we can each be "right" in our own way.
    - Be vulnerable and receptive to feedback.

CHAPTER 10

Manage Your Time, Manage Your Life

Be prepared. It's better to be proactive than reactive.

Lesson 1: Life is a marathon, not a sprint.

Some days I feel stressed, reactive, frustrated, and impatient. It all feels like too much—kids screaming, no one wants the meal I cooked, toys everywhere, dishes in the sink, emails waiting, babysitters canceling, and daddy needs attention too. Life can be overwhelming.

What would my mom say? "Take a deep breath. Nothing is wrong; you are okay. This is life—imperfectly perfect. You are doing great. It *is* challenging, and you *can* handle it. Just breathe."

When I'm in a reactive state, the idea of pausing to get proactive can certainly seem challenging, but I've learned that a simple pause can make a huge difference regarding the degree of urgency I unnecessarily put on myself.

Manage your energy. Just like a marathon, managing daily life requires considerable energy. Just because we made it through one day successfully does *not* mean we are done. Every day our family must eat, sleep, and simply exist. At the end of the day, when we are exhausted and all we want is our child to fall asleep, will we have enough energy left to be patient through the process?

Time management is one of the most important skills for managing our energy. When we create a plan each day, we can simply follow the plan. And although it may seem more controlling initially, it can actually feel more freeing in the moment.

Whether it's bills, work, health, or meal planning, there are certain daily tasks that must be accomplished. Life is maintenance. For example, brushing teeth. Most of us don't think, "Ugh, really? *Again*?" Most of us understand it is something that we will be doing forever.

So, how to make repetitive processes as hassle-free as brushing teeth; how to create a routine that feels manageable and easy? The answer is to *prepare*.

Systematize repetitive tasks. If you have something that you must do each day, week, or month, create a system so you don't have to rethink each time you do it. For example, my mom had copies of a universal grocery list with all the items we ever bought. It was her way to remember all the meals she could cook, and all the products we used at home. When an item was finished, she'd mark it on the list. By using this list, she would always know what needed to be replaced and also have a reference for meal planning each week.

My husband used to make fun of me at the beginning of our relationship for my lack of systemization. At the time I was working three jobs, and each night I would calculate what time I had to wake up the following morning, while he thought it should already have been decided: Mondays I wake up at one time, Tuesdays, another, etc. It soon became obvious to me as well that I wouldn't need to think about this every day if I planned out my morning routines, and then consistently followed that plan.

Going to the gym, or remembering to meditate, are exactly the same. Rather than thinking about how or when to go to the gym each day, put it on the weekly schedule; a daily meditation schedule can also be a valuable tool.

Don't procrastinate. In addition to systemizing daily and weekly tasks, it's important not to procrastinate. If you address small tasks when they arise, they won't pile up into daunting projects. My mom used to say, "It takes thirty seconds to either re-hang or put your worn clothes in the hamper, but it will take much longer to clean a messy room."

Mail is another good example of something that, if left undealt with, will pile up. One of the daily practices I use to help maintain an absence of clutter is to open all my mail before I walk into my house, so I can just throw out the envelopes and add the bills to my to-do list. It takes one minute in that moment rather than dealing with a daunting pile at the end of the week or month.

Life is easier when we approach tasks with baby steps. If we consistently do small tasks, we can get the satisfaction of completion, and we can move on to the next task. Even if it is a large task, it can be broken down into smaller bites. Take this book, for example; it is much less daunting to write when I focus on one section at a time. The moment I start to think about the entire project, I am left intimidated and unmotivated. When I set realistic expectations of what I can achieve in each circumstance, I am setting myself up for success; whereas unrealistic expectations lead to unnecessary pressure, stress, and procrastination.

Lesson 2: Be organized.

As a student in grade school I remember learning time-management skills from my mom. She would help me look at the big picture of all my school work, assist me by dividing it into smaller tasks, and create a plan and schedule for how and when to do each small piece of the whole. Like this process, the following practices still create the foundation of my days.

1. Keep an ongoing to-do list.
   - A. Every time you think of something you want to do, write it down (in one place!). This way your mind doesn't have to remember everything and has more space to be present.
2. Clarify daily/weekly/monthly priorities.
   - A. If you had a bucket and wanted to fill it with the most sand, pebbles, and rocks possible, you would put the rocks in first, then pebbles, and then the sand. If you filled the bucket first with sand, there would be less room for everything else.
   - B. Your time is your bucket, and your priorities are your rocks—if you don't put them in first, you won't have time for them.
   - C. Some examples of priorities include:
     - ✦ Self-care.
       - Exercise x times per week.
       - Meditate x times per week.
     - ✦ Relationship Maintenance.
       - Quality time with people x times per week or month.

3. Keep a Calendar.
   A. Fill your calendar with your rocks/priorities first.
   B. Put repetitive activities such as your wake up/breakfast routine, exercise, meditation, drop off and pick up from school, playtime, naptime, dinnertime, bedtime, etc., in the calendar on repeat.
   C. By following the above, you can easily see the buckets of available free time.
   D. Be sure to take items from your to-do list and put them in the buckets of free time.

4. Prepare for the following day.
   A. Every night before bed look at your calendar, make necessary updates, and be mentally prepared for the following day.
   B. If, during the day, you can't get to one of your scheduled activities, move it to a free bucket of time on another day. It's okay to be adaptable—just try not to let your priorities get pushed out of the schedule.

In summary, when we are organized, we can manage our energy, systematize repetitive tasks, and be better prepared for each day. It takes self-discipline and effort, but when we are proactive, and make sure our needs are met, we can be less reactive—which makes parenting a lot easier!

Remember

1. Life is a marathon, not a sprint.
   - A. Manage your energy.
   - B. Systematize repetitive tasks.
   - C. Don't procrastinate.
     - ✦ Deal with things when they are small, so they won't pile up.
     - ✦ Unrealistic expectations lead to unnecessary pressure, stress, and failure.

2. Be organized.
   - A. Keep a to-do list.
   - B. Clarify priorities.
   - C. Keep a calendar.
     - ✦ Put your priorities in the calendar first.
     - ✦ Add to-do list items to free time when necessary.
   - D. Prepare for the following day.

PART 2

Live from Love - Start Within

Nurture Your Mind, Heart, Body, & Soul

As I continue on my path as a mother, I can't help but compare myself to my mom. Sometimes I think about how much more patient or fun she was than me, and I put pressure on myself to live up to the pedestal on which I placed her.

I aspire to be an extraordinary mommy, like she was. I aspire to access the extraordinary me I believe I was destined to be, in all areas of my life. But when I am exhausted, stressed, overworked, spread too thin, I don't feel extraordinary at all and it is much more difficult to have the inner strength to do the things I have written about in this book.

To be as present, patient, loving, and connected as I strive to be, effort is required. Inner peace doesn't come naturally. I wouldn't expect to be physically fit if I never exercised, so why assume I'll be mentally, emotionally, or spiritually fit without effort?

Our presence as mothers is the foundation of the home, and *how* we show up influences how everyone else responds. If we are okay, they will be okay. Therefore, self-care is the first non-negotiable.

Life is like a building. If it is built without a solid foundation, eventually it will crumble. *Self-care is our foundation. It is a necessity, not only a luxury.*

My mom knew this. Her ability to do the practices in this book with ease and grace was because she put her own well-being above all. She had enough love to give to us because she was not running on empty; she filled up her own love tank every single day.

Self-care practices aren't as effective when practiced only every now and then, on a whim, or after we've eaten too much. They need to be the infrastructure of our life. Other parts of our life can be scheduled around the time we make for ourselves, which benefits both us and our family. More importantly, *there is no need to feel guilty about taking care of ourselves.* When you take care of you, you are a stronger rock for everyone else.

I never questioned the time my mom took for self-care. It didn't bother me, and I didn't feel she was guilty of neglecting us in any way. It was understood that this was part of the daily routine; a set boundary, just like bedtime. We always understood that when mom was good, everyone was good.

CHAPTER 11

Manage Your Mind

Self-criticism and doubt clutters the mind.
Be your own cheerleader.

Lesson 1: Be kind to yourself.

After my daughter was born, I noticed myself fishing for compliments. I wanted validation. I wanted to be told that it was legitimate that I was exhausted, and that I was doing a great job balancing two kids for the first time. I wanted someone to say that I was crazy for feeling guilty that I wasn't being more "productive"—that the work I was doing was far more important than any task on a to-do list.

Yet, even when someone told me those things, I didn't believe them. I was unknowingly being quite hard on myself. I was comparing myself to an unachievable ideal.

What would my mom have said to this self-critical voice in my head? "My sweet, darling daughter, are you kidding? Do you see all that you are doing? You are balancing so much. You are nursing around the clock, you haven't slept more than three hours straight, and you share your huge smile and give your undivided attention when you are with your kids. How crazy to think you aren't doing enough!"

Although at first I thought I needed my husband to compliment me more to make up for this perceived lack of positive feedback, I ultimately remembered that *my self-talk is my responsibility.*

Now that I'm writing this book, my inner critic is especially mean. "You don't even do all these practices consistently with your kids. You aren't an extraordinary parent. Remember that time when you were on your phone, or that other time when you weren't fully engaged!?"

In response, I breathe deeply and remember that I am imperfectly perfect. That being extraordinary doesn't mean I have to be flawless. My extraordinary is my commitment to *be love*, to commit to my personal growth, and notice and improve the moments I can.

I always do my best to remember I am human, not a robot.

It is important to be self-reflective and passionate about personal growth, but it isn't necessary to be mean to yourself in the process. How you talk to yourself affects how you feel. How you feel affects how you treat others—especially your kids.

Here are some important steps for improving self-talk:

1. *Identify.* Start to notice inner chatter of self-doubt or criticism. Imagine you had someone berating you all day, every day. How would you feel? Horrible. The self-hating voice in your head is like a bully from which you cannot hide. Somehow it thinks that being critical will motivate you to be better, but in truth, it just makes you feel bad.

2. *Personify.* Make this inner bully into a character. Give it a name, a face, and an image; then start to disconnect from it as your true voice. How do you know it's not your true voice? If it was you, you would be able to shut it up! This voice is on autopilot, and likely originated in your childhood as some

form of protection—but you *can* disidentify with it because it no longer serves you.

3. *Acknowledge.* We don't negotiate with terrorists. Your inner bully could be telling you something clearly true, like "your hair is brown." It doesn't matter if the bully is accurate. If the sentiment is not loving, there is no reason to engage. You don't have to tell the bully a positive perspective. You don't have to change its viewpoint. Simply become present and acknowledge that this negative voice exists, as you lovingly remember that *it* is not in charge.
4. *Accept.* What? Accept it? How is that possible?! Why would I want to accept this "terrible" (don't judge!) part of me? Loving acceptance is the only way it will start to subside. Remember, those who are hardest to love, need love the most—and we must begin with ourselves. Once you start to acknowledge and disassociate from your inner bully, you can begin to create a loving relationship with it. Remember that *loving your inner bully doesn't mean liking it*, it means unconditionally accepting that it exists. Just like a hug, this loving acceptance allows the negativity to dissipate because darkness cannot exist in light.
5. *Release.* Once we accept its presence, its strength starts to lessen. Here are a few strategies to help release the negative commentary of the inner bully:
   - Tell yourself, "It's okay to let it go. You don't need it anymore," and just watch the voice drift away.
   - Treat it like a small child. "I love you but I'm not listening to you." If a child was having a tantrum and you yelled, kicked, and told her she was horrible, would it help? No. It would make her feel worse.

- ✦ Pause, breathe, and speak to the inner bully as if giving a hurt child a loving hug: "You are okay. I am here. I love you."
- ✦ Remember, just because we think something, doesn't mean it's true.

6. *Praise.* Be your own cheerleader. In addition to commending ourselves for the little external victories in life, it's important to celebrate the triumphs in our head as well. Every moment we do any of the steps above, *we are improving our self-talk.* Praising these simple moments reinforces the process and begins to create a stronger foundation.
7. *Practice.* Developing a new relationship with our inner-bully takes time, just like learning a new language; we don't start speaking fluently after only one attempt. Be patient with yourself. Think about how many years this voice has been in charge. These patterns of the mind have strong groundwork that needs to be chipped away, one moment at a time.
8. *Repeat.* When we are kind to ourselves, we are kinder to those around us, especially our children (and hopefully to our partners too!)

Remember

1. Be kind to yourself.
   A. Identify.
      - Identify negative self-talk.
   B. Personify.
      - Make your "inner bully" its own character.
   C. Acknowledge.
      - Notice *how* your inner bully talks to you, not what it's saying.
      - Don't negotiate with it.
   D. Accept.
      - Lovingly accept that the bully is there.
   E. Release.
      - Tell yourself it's okay to let go. The bully's words are not your truth; you don't need the negativity anymore.
   F. Praise.
      - Celebrate the moments when you do any of the steps above.
      - This praise creates a new foundation of self-love.
   G. Practice.
      - Be patient with yourself. Developing a new relationship with your inner-bully takes time, just ike learning a new language.
   H. Repeat.

CHAPTER 12

Heal Your Heart

Our feelings are our responsibility.
Our kids don't deserve our pain.

Lesson 1: Our feelings are our own responsibility.

It pains me to say it, but I can understand how people can hurt their children. I've had moments where it takes every ounce of my strength to refrain from doing or saying the terrible things that are raging inside me. It scares me. I want to blame my kids and tell them they are "making" me act this way. I want them to fix it—to fix me. Those moments are red flags that there are deeper issues that I need to address.

Of course, it's okay to occasionally become upset. We are human. We can't help how we feel. Feelings come and go as they please. The challenge is *not to stop feeling*. It is *how to better handle feelings*. Just like the inner bully, if we can stay present and loving toward difficult feelings then they don't have to be in charge.

Children are deeply in tune with the non-verbal cues they receive from others. If we are anxious, frustrated, stressed, or angry, guess what? They feel it. Ever wonder why kids are more difficult to manage when we are stressed out? It's because they feed off our energy. Even if we put on a smile and do our best to stay outwardly patient, they still feel what we feel. Feelings are contagious.

And, unfortunately, when we need self-care the most, it is often prioritized the least. People think when things get easier then they'll work on themselves, whereas the opposite is true—*it is when we work on ourselves that things will become easier.*

Many feelings, like anxiety, fear, sadness, etc., can be habitual responses that were ingrained within us over time. But with intention and practice, these emotional habits can be unraveled and released.

I once had a client who told me she didn't have the "luxury to break down." She had to "hold it all together" or her world would shatter. Interestingly, by not dealing with her feelings, they came out in other ways. Maybe she didn't cry all the time, but she did drink a lot.

Negative behaviors are a result of not dealing with feelings. When we don't address our feelings in a healthy way, we often develop unhealthy behaviors to compensate, and we may *overdo* certain things like eating, drinking, shopping, sexing, or exercising—behaviors that can arise from an inability to deal with feelings healthily.

Lesson 2: Deal with feelings in a healthy way.

What does this mean? It is important not to *avoid* feelings, but to *embrace* them as part of your wholeness—your perfection. Beautiful feelings can be enjoyed, and challenging feelings can lead to growth. With that said, feelings are complex. While there are myriads of books and lifetimes of therapy that deal with these complexities, here I will offer some basics:

There are three ways that people generally deal with uncomfortable feelings:

Self-medication: People often use external sources to "calm" themselves or make themselves feel "better" temporarily. Examples include food, alcohol, shopping, drugs, sex, etc. However, the temporary high often leaves you with more negative feelings, such as guilt, shame, frustration, and self-criticism. Then the cycle continues. You feel worse, then engage in the behavior again to make yourself feel "better."

Distraction: Since feelings can be "uncomfortable," people often try not to feel them. Consciously or unconsciously, they find methods of distraction such as work or screens to keep their minds occupied and ignore what is going on within.

Engulfment: If someone is screaming, they may be overtaken by anger. If someone is controlling, they may be overtaken by anxiety. Sometimes feelings are so intense that we can get enveloped in them.

What to do instead:

1. If you tend to become engulfed in feelings in a way that doesn't serve you:
   A. In the moment, *Focus Outward.* Notice the feelings taking over. Bring yourself to the present moment around you. Because feelings can be stronger than thoughts, specific efforts to become aware of your surroundings can pull you out of the feeling. Use your senses to:
      - *Listen.* Notice the sounds in the background.
      - *Touch.* Caress your hand or arm gently.
      - *See.* Get out of your head and identify items in your environment.
      - *Breathe.* Focus on deep, belly breathing.

B. Afterward, *Reflect*. Take time to think about what happened.

- ✦ What were you feeling?
- ✦ What triggered your feelings to take over so strongly?
- ✦ Are there other ways you could approach these triggers in the future?
- ✦ Are there ways to be better prepared for them?

2. If you tend to distract or self-medicate, instead:

A. In the moment, *Focus Inward*. If you notice yourself engaging in destructive behaviors like overeating, drinking, "sneaky shopping," etc., then pause, breathe, and start to pay attention to what is going on inside you. What are you feeling? What does your heart need? Give yourself permission to feel.

- ✦ Open yourself to fully experiencing your feelings.
- ✦ Lean into the feelings and allow them to move through you.
- ✦ If possible, journal or talk to someone about your feelings.
- ✦ Cry. Scream. Whatever you need to let yourself feel. (Not at someone, but perhaps with someone.)
- ✦ Experience whatever is going on within you, without judgment.

B. Afterward, *Reflect*. Take time to think about what happened.

- ✦ What is difficult or scary about letting yourself feel?
- ✦ What is your resistance to letting yourself feel?

- What would it take to be more open to your feelings?
- What would it take to accept that they are part of your perfection?
- *Challenging feelings are our teachers; they identify opportunities for reflection and growth.*

When we understand these concepts, it becomes easier to deal with our feelings. Here is a synopsis of how to deal with feelings in a healthy way:

1. Be aware.
    - What are you feeling?
2. Get present.
    - If a feeling is engulfing you in a way that doesn't serve you, bring yourself into the stillness of the present moment. *Focus Outward.*
    - If you are distracting or "self-medicating," focus on letting yourself feel your feelings. *Focus Inward.*
3. Lovingly accept.
    - The goal is *not* to get rid of the uncomfortable feelings; it is to lovingly accept them.
        - When someone feels loved, they feel relaxed. When your feelings are loved and accepted, they can relax too!
4. Learn.
    - *Reflect.* Think about what you can learn about yourself from your feelings.

When my mom died I felt an intensity of emotions that I had not experienced before. I had a small child, my own business, a marriage, a new home that was under a full renovation, and my devastated, depressed father for whom I felt responsible. In this circumstance many would undoubtedly say, "I must hold it all together. I need to push these feelings down and take care of everything and everyone else." But as much as it was a priority to take care of all of these other aspects of my life, I knew that I had to take care of myself first.

But because I was *aware* of how much pain I was experiencing within, and understood it wasn't appropriate to be overtaken by my feelings all day every day, I made sure to allocate time to *be present* with my feelings. For example, I would go to spin class and ride a bike in the back of the dark room while crying my eyes out. While my son napped I would meditate, journal, or read books about death and dying. I *lovingly accepted* all the feelings that arose within me. As painful as they were, I didn't want them to go away. I wasn't frustrated that six months later the intensity was still as strong as day one, but accepted the process with no expectations of what was to come. I embraced my feelings and opened myself up to the gifts I would *learn* from this experience.

Obviously, this is a more intense experience than most people experience daily. Whether you are dealing with something serious or just the ups and downs of life, it is helpful to have a consistent practice to deal with your feelings.

For more details on how to handle feelings in a healthy way, you can read my other book, *Extraordinary You: Master Your Feelings, Master Your Life*.

Lesson 3: Develop a simple daily/weekly practice.

Think of feelings as being like dirty laundry—which piles up when ignored— it's much easier to deal with feelings as they come rather than to deal with all of them later. Creating a practice that we can do every day, for the rest of our life, helps us manage our "inner laundry."

1. Some suggestions include:
   - Seeing a therapist.
   - Journaling for five minutes a day.
   - Making five minutes of "reflection time" a few times a week.
   - Meditating for at least one minute a day.
2. If you don't know how to meditate or journal, or have a stigma against therapy, those are *great excuses to do nothing.* In this case, exploring that feeling of *resistance* is a good place to start.
3. Doing something is better than doing nothing.

Remember

1. Your feelings are your responsibility.
   - A. The challenge is *not* to stop feeling; it is to better handle your feelings.
   - B. When you work on yourself, things will get easier.
   - C. Self-destructive behaviors are a result of not dealing with feelings.
2. Overview of healthy ways to deal with feelings:
   - A. Be aware.
     - ✦ What are you feeling?
   - B. Be present.
     - ✦ *Engulfment*: Focus outward instead; observe your surroundings and use your senses in the present moment.
     - ✦ *Distraction or self-medication*: Focus inward instead; then feel your feelings.
     - ✦ *Lovingly accept*.
     - ✦ *Learn*. What can you learn from your feelings?
3. Develop a simple daily/weekly practice:
   - A. Possibilities include therapy, journaling, meditation, exercise.
   - B. Notice the desire to come up with excuses.
   - C. Doing something is better than doing nothing.

CHAPTER 13

Bless Your Body

Your body wants to be healthy.
Learn to listen to it.

Lesson 1: Listen to your body.

My relationship with food and my body went through some serious challenges in my adolescence and early twenties. It is tremendously difficult to have a solid sense of self when you live in a society that values physicality (and wealth, power, drama, and fame) over intelligence, goodness, and connectedness.

Before my mom's passing, my relationship with my body was the biggest internal struggle that I faced, and eventually conquered. At my lowest moments I would restrict my food intake, binge, over-exercise, and repeat—getting stuck in the vicious cycle of letting my happiness depend on how fat I felt in any given moment. Years of journaling and self-reflection got me through this difficult time.

What did I learn? Trust in nature. Trust that your body wants to be healthy. Bodies have mechanisms within that tell us what they need and when they're satisfied. All we need do is notice them. Seems easy enough, but why is it actually so difficult? Because most people prefer not to have to pay attention within and would rather be distracted.

If you listen to the whispers of your body, it won't have to scream. As a teenager I was intense about my exercise routine. I had to work out hard. I had to sweat to burn calories. I would poke fun at my mom who could wear the same gym clothes all week since she didn't break a sweat. She wasn't pushing, and that confused me. So how did she stay so healthy without trying harder? She listened to her body. She ate consciously. She found an exercise routine that was hard enough to keep her healthy, but easy enough that she could do it consistently.

Give your body what it needs, rather than trying to control it. For our bodies to be healthy, we must move them regularly. Create a comfortable exercise routine that can be maintained long term, rather than pushing too hard for a certain period of time and then quitting!

Consistency is key. It's important not to try to control our weight. Rather than restricting our food intake by focusing on what we can't have, actually focusing on what we *can* have, and the ways it will nourish our body, is the best approach. Develop healthy and consistent practices that can be maintained, and avoid quick fixes. Exercise with *consistency* as the intention, not weight loss.

Lesson 2: Eat consciously.

How we eat is as important as what we eat. Most people who struggle with food and body issues focus on *what* they are eating more than on *how* they are eating. As important as it is to make eating plant-based, non-processed foods a priority, eating some yummy garbage is okay too every now and again—if you enjoy it and eat it consciously.

What does eating consciously look like?

1. *When you feel like eating, pause for a moment and look within* to see if it is your "*mouth*" *or your* "*stomach*" that is in need.
   A. Does my mouth want food, or is my body actually hungry?
      - ✦ "*Mouth*." Sometimes we feel like eating, but we're not actually hungry.
        - *Emotional avoi*dance can trigger the desire to eat. We want the sensation, or the distraction of eating so we don't have to deal with internal discomfort.
          - ~ If you use food when avoiding emotions, try to see the desire to eat as a red flag that you have feelings that need your love and attention.
        - *Enjoyment*. Other times, a food just looks yummy and we want to taste it.
          - ~ If you are eating for the pure satisfaction of the flavors, notice them. When your tongue is done tasting, you might be tempted to eat faster and take bigger bites to get back the satisfaction of the first bite. Once this starts happening it means you are finished, and you *won't* get any additional pleasure from eating more.
      - ✦ "*Stomach*." If you are eating because your body is hungry, in addition to tasting the food, notice the sensations in your stomach. Pay attention to when you feel full, then stop.
2. *Bless your food*. I find that this practice helps me breathe deeply and become present before eating. Take time to

feel grateful. Think about how the food got to your plate. Acknowledge the time, people, history, and life that went into making your food possible. For example, think about a banana: How long did it take to grow? Who picked it? What did they go through to pick that banana? How did it get to the store? What has happened historically so that many of us don't plant and pick our own food? When I started taking a moment to bless my food every time I ate everything changed for me; I became present enough to truly enjoy eating rather than continuing a mindless act of emotional avoidance.

3. *Take deep breaths before you eat.* Slow down. Sometimes our excited anticipation of eating, or even just the rush of life, makes eating a very fast and mindless process. Taking a few breaths can help us to become more aware of the act of eating, which also can help us to become more aware of when we feel full.

4. *Do nothing else.* Don't watch TV, look at your phone, or eat on the go. Sit down, pay attention, and enjoy each bite.

5. *Eat with your family.* These are practices that can be done with your family. Meal time can be a time to be together, to be present and grateful to be eating, and to bond with one another. Studies show that families who eat meals together are more connected and have healthier relationships.

The practice of eating consciously has not only kept me at my ideal body weight, but it has allowed me to eat what I want without trying to control my body. This practice is particularly helpful when going through the weight changes, both gain and loss, associated with pregnancy.

Lesson 3: Be kind to yourself. (Another reminder!)

When we are mean to ourselves, we feel bad. When we feel bad, we engage in unhealthy behaviors. When we are kind to ourselves, the unhealthy behaviors naturally subside. I have multiple clients who lost up to fifty pounds simply by changing their self-talk.

Rather than making rules for what you should or shouldn't do, focus on listening to what your body is really telling you. Trust the process of listening to your body rather than focusing on controlling yourself to achieve an outcome. For example, I do my best to eat consciously when my stomach is hungry or if there is something yummy to taste. I don't have rules about calories or eating at specific times of the day. If I start eating and I don't taste the food, it's my red flag to stop. If I'm enjoying the food, but my stomach feels full, it's also my indication that the meal is over. I try to listen to the signs my body is telling me.

To be kinder to yourself, try the following:

1. Stop trying to control.
    - When I told myself I *shouldn't* eat something, it made me want it more.
    - When I told myself I needed to lose weight, I wanted to eat more.
    - When I told myself I should exercise harder, I resisted going to the gym.
    - When I told myself I was fat, I felt bad and was more critical of myself or others.
    - When I told myself I'd eat less at my next meal, it was a red flag that I wanted to overeat even though I was full.

2. Listen to your body's physical cues; trust that it wants to be healthy.

3. Strengthen beliefs that help you trust your body. For example:
    - ✦ My body doesn't want to be over or underweight. If I trust and listen to its signals, it will return to its ideal and natural state.
    - ✦ I can eat whatever I want *if* I listen to my body's cues that tell me when I'm done, and I eat consciously and fully *enjoy* eating.
    - ✦ My body is not me. It is a vessel. When I die my body will remain, and I will not. While I'm living in my body, I must love, appreciate, and care for it.

When gaining and losing baby weight, I stuck with these practices. I listened to my body, ate consciously, and was kind to myself. I continued to exercise daily and didn't try to control or restrict my healthy food intake. With no extra action, the weight came on and then fell off.

In the moments when the weight wasn't coming off as "fast" as I wanted, I was quick to notice the desire to control. I remembered to come back to my practice and to *listen to my body rather than focus on my desired results*. It can be challenging to feel uncomfortable in your own skin, and to not like what your body looks or feels like—but being controlling and mean to yourself will make matters worse, not better. The more you understand yourself, the more you understand how to listen to what your body is telling you.

Remember

1. Listen to your body.
   A. *If you listen to the whispers of your body, it won't have to scream.*
      ✦ Give your body what it needs. Don't try to control it.
      ✦ Exercise with consistency as the intention, not weight gain or loss.
2. Eat consciously.
   A. *How you eat is as important as what you eat.*
      ✦ When you feel like eating, pause and notice where the desire comes from.
      ✦ Is it your "mouth" wanting food?
         • Are you avoiding feelings?
            ~ Desire to eat is a red flag that you have feelings that need your love and attention.
         • Do you just want to enjoy something yummy?
            ~ Taste each bite and stop when the satisfaction is done.
      ✦ Is your body hungry?
         • When your stomach is sufficiently full, you are done.
   B. Bless your food.
   C. Take deep breaths before you eat.
   D. Do nothing else. *Eat without distractions, screens, etc.*
3. Be kind to yourself.
   A. Stop trying to control.
   B. Listen to your body's cues; trust that it wants to be healthy.
   C. Strengthen beliefs that help you to trust your body.

CHAPTER 14

Be Love

Who you are is as important as what you do.
Leave a legacy of love.

Lesson 1: Love unapologetically.

Sometimes I was embarrassed by my mom. She would often hug for too long or hold someone's face while telling them something special. Her gifts were often over-the-top, like a three-foot-tall teddy bear for a baby whose family lived in a tiny New York City apartment. I told her she didn't respect people's personal space; that she didn't pay attention to whether someone was open to receiving her love. I told her she was being selfish by doing something that made her feel good; that she wasn't paying attention to whether her intense hug and face holding were invited.

She was open to receiving my feedback. Like always, she reflected on it, and in this circumstance, she changed nothing. She didn't agree. She simply loved unapologetically. She didn't care how uncomfortable people seemed in the moment, or how unusual it was that she was affectionate toward strangers. She didn't agree with the norm. She didn't agree that people should act like they didn't care about one another. She knew that deep down everyone wanted love. She made it her job to share it because she was overflowing with it. She knew that there was absolutely *nothing more important in this life than being love.* I now believe she was right.

After she was gone, people spoke on and on about how she made them feel. No one talked about her successful jewelry business, her significant education, the many languages she spoke, the countries she visited, or her sculptures and artwork. Everyone talked about how they felt when they were with her. They felt alive. They felt seen. They felt heard. They felt loved.

Those who "had no room" for an oversized teddy bear were forever grateful that their child had the biggest, most special friend. Those whom she hugged too tightly realized that before Betsy they were giving wimpy hugs. Those whose faces she held to tell them how important they were in this world never forgot that moment.

My mom was never embarrassed to love, even if it wasn't "appropriate." When I told her that her email address with the username "Bighugs4u" wasn't professional, and that she shouldn't use it to deal with official matters, she simply responded with "Professionals need hugs too."

Just like all children lucky enough to have their mother's love, *my mom's love was the foundation of my life.* I am blessed that she was so good at it. My brother and I were the recipients of the most intense, pure, unconditional love that one can imagine. She accepted our flaws. She saw our weaknesses and shortcomings as an opportunity for reflection and learning. She would always make sure to differentiate, "Just because I didn't like what you did, never means that I don't love *you*."

We parents are the leaders of love in our homes. How we love will affect who our children become. Please don't let the storms of life keep you from experiencing the sunshine. You are light. You are love.

Lesson 2: Love is the source of everything.

When in doubt, *always return to love.* If you don't know what to do, just ask yourself, "How can I *be* love in this circumstance? What would love do now?" Rather than love as a verb, think of love as a state of being.

To "be love" means to:

- Use positive reinforcement. Showering all things done well with praise will encourage more things to be done well.
- Never, ever be critical. If someone messes up, you can be disappointed (but don't try to inspire guilt in them!) or concerned—just remember that being mean or aggressive is not helpful.
- Always treat others as teammates, never as opponents.
- See failure as opportunity for growth so your kids won't need to fear it.
- Remember life's challenges are gifts; opportunities to learn and evolve.
- Read between the lines. See negative behavior as a symptom of deeper hurt.
- Everyone has a different perspective. Assume the good in people, even when they don't see it in themselves.
- There is always more to every story. Don't jump to conclusions.
- Lead with love, not fear. There is no reason to fear people's judgments.
- It doesn't hurt to speak up. Ask for what you want. Be strong yet soft.
- Love conquers all. Hug and kiss with no boundaries. Always tell people you love them.
- Let gratitude flow through your veins. Whenever something goes wrong, be empathetic to the challenging circumstance

and then say "At least ..." as you find something for which to be grateful. "At least we are all together."

- Don't complain. Rather than "I have to ..." think "I get to ...." Remember that most of the things people complain about are luxuries to many people in this world. "I get to change my child's dirty diaper. I get to wake up with my baby in the middle of the night."
- Don't take things for granted, and remember, it could always be worse.
- Know you are blessed.

Lesson 3: Create a spiritual practice.

How was my mom able to love like this? She was a unique specimen, someone who was unquestionably "plugged in" to the divine, and highly committed to that deeper connection. She believed that if she was spiritually connected then everything else would fall into place.

Growing up my friends would ask, "What is your mom doing?"

"She is meditating," I would reply.

"What's that?"

"It's kind of like sleeping," I'd say. "She sits quietly and that makes her happier. Doesn't your mom do that too?"

My mom allocated at least an hour every single day to meditating. Whether she woke up thirty minutes early and went to bed thirty minutes later, she prioritized it. It wasn't always simple; I remember sitting at the airport, waiting for the plane to arrive, and mom would let us know she was going to meditate for a bit. We knew that when she was meditating we had to occupy ourselves.

Surprising to me, *my mom started her spiritual journey later in life*, in her early thirties, right before she had me. At that time, she found a spiritual teacher who taught the spiritual teachings of Light and Sound Current. She learned to meditate, read books, took courses, and did recommended exercises. She was fascinated with the journey of the soul, death, afterlife, and oneness. She became tremendously committed to evolving and expanding her connection to spirit. She understood that the only part of life that was inevitable was death, and that comfort with and acceptance of mortality was integral in living more fully.

She worked with this same teacher for over thirty years. Sometimes I was jealous of him. I would question her about him. I didn't like that she followed him with so much faith. She received my concerns with love and explained to me that he was just the messenger. Her spiritual practice didn't have anything to do with him specifically; it was what she learned through him. I finally got it when she pointed out that, who she was as a person and a mother, came from his teachings. It didn't matter if I liked him, or even if she liked him. What she learned by being guided on her own spiritual journey was the foundation of my blessed life.

Not only did she share what she learned through open conversation and modeling, but she would also *meditate each night with us before bed.* We would visualize a column of light and relinquish our worries and fears into it; we took a moment to feel gratitude and to send blessings to those we love.

It doesn't matter whether it's a spiritual practice like hers, or a more religious approach, as long as it is based in love. *Many roads lead to the source.* However, it is easy to get caught up in the waves of life if you don't have a spiritual practice that grounds you to the stillness of the ocean floor.

Remember

1. Love unapologetically.
   - A parent's love is the foundation of a child's life.
2. Love is the source of everything.
   - Don't be critical; use positive reinforcement.
   - Treat people as teammates, not opponents.
   - There is no such thing as failure, just opportunities to learn and grow.
   - Read between the lines; negative behavior is a symptom of something deeper.
   - Everyone has a different perspective; we can all be "right."
   - Don't jump to conclusions.
   - Assume the good in people.
   - It never hurts to ask.
   - Be strong yet soft.
   - Be grateful. Say "At least ..." and find something to appreciate.
   - Rather than "I have to ..." say "I get to ...."
   - Hug and kiss with no boundaries.
   - Always tell people you love them.

3. Create a spiritual practice.
    - It's never too late to develop a spiritual practice.
    - Add a spiritual practice to your children's bedtime ritual.
    - Many roads lead to the source.

Dear Mommy

As this labor of love comes to an end, I want to send a note out into the universe to my beloved mommy ... wherever she is.

Mommy, I miss you more than words can express. There are moments when I still can't believe you are no longer here. It instantly brings tears to my eyes to realize it. Although I can't touch you, I know you are still with me; I feel you. When I let myself experience that connection, my fears and self-doubt subside, and I trust that everything is precisely as it is supposed to be.

I can't remember most of the monotonous days or the routines we had growing up, but I have so many random special memories, full of giggles, that resulted from your dedication to making life special and fun. *Thank you for being wise enough to be silly.* You knew that life was temporary, and you taught us to enjoy it. I am forever grateful for that.

Even without your physical presence, I am amazed that every day I manage to feel more loved by you. How profound, that the more deeply I fall in love with my own children, the more I understand the depth of your love for me. Thank you.

I feel so blessed to experience your strength, wisdom, support, and joy as I follow in your footsteps to embrace your most treasured role in life ...

"Mom."

About the Author

Jasmin Terrany, LMHC

Like most mothers, Jasmin wears many hats. With two master's degrees from Columbia University, she has not only built a thriving Life Therapy practice, but she is also a speaker, author, wife, sister, daughter, friend, and fellow human. Most importantly, she is a mommy to her precious children Liv and Zen.

As a Libra, she is inspired to balance it all. She is devoted to live from love—to learn in challenging times, to have courage to speak her truth, to lead with faith not fear, to give unconditionally, to enjoy simple moments, and to have as much silly fun as possible.

To learn more about Jasmin,
visit her website: www.JasminBalance.com

Resources

Priscilla Dunstan on Oprah:
https://www.youtube.com/watch?v=PgkZf6jVdVg

Ted Talk: *What Makes a Good Life? Lessons from the Longest Study on Happiness*
https://www.ted.com/talks/robert_waldinger_what_makes_a_good_life_lessons_from_the_longest_study_on_happiness

***Daniel Tiger's Neighborhood* on PBS Kids**
My favorite children's show to teach emotional intelligence.

Available at www.JasminBalance.com:

✦ Other Books in the *Be Extraordinary Series*

- **Extraordinary You:** *Master Your Feelings, Master Your Life The Four Essential Exercises that Build Emotional Resilience & Enduring Confidence.*
    - ~ This book does a deep dive into the concepts discussed in Chapter 12: *Heal Your Heart.*
- *Childhood Bedtime Meditation:* I created a guided recording of the meditation my mom did with us each night.

In Memory of Mom

Elisabeth "Betsy" Tanjeloff
The Light of Our Lives
January 31, 1950 - Infinity